STEPHEN DOUDS is a television producer for BBC Northern Ireland's award-winning factual department. He has made programmes in locations as diverse as Israel, New York, the Vatican and France, and has produced various documentaries and features for BBC Radio 2 and Radio 4. He is a critic and reviewer for various publications, including the *Irish Times*, and is a Trustee of the Lyric Theatre and of the Irish Association. He lives in south Belfast.

STEPHEN DOUDS

THE
BELFAST
BLITZ

BLACKSTAFF
PRESS
BELFAST

First published in 2011 by
Blackstaff Press
4c Heron Wharf, Sydenham Business Park
Belfast, BT3 9LE
with the assistance of
The Arts Council of Northern Ireland

The acknowledgements on pages 157–166 constitute
an extension of this copyright page

Designed and Typeset by CJWT Solutions, St Helens

Printed in Belfast by W&G Baird Limited, County Antrim

A CIP catalogue record for this book
is available from the British Library

ISBN 978 0 85640 863 2

www.blackstaffpress.com

Pro Tanto Quid Retribuamus
For so much, what shall we give in return?

CONTENTS

MINISTRY OF PUBLIC SECURITY

EVACUATION OF SCHOOL CHILDREN

The Evacuation of School Children from Belfast will begin on SUNDAY NEXT, JULY 7th

Further announcements will be made in the Press and by Posters outside Schools on SATURDAY

ONLY REGISTERED EVACUEES WILL BE DEALT WITH ON SUNDAY. They should assemble at the Places and Times stated on their personal Assembly Instruction Sheets.

UNREGISTERED CHILDREN in the Area covered by the Schools named below will be Evacuated on **MONDAY, JULY 8th:—**

BEECHFIELD	MEGAIN MEMORIAL	ST. MALACHY'S
BELVOIR HALL	MEMEL STREET	BOYS' (NEW LODGE ROAD)
BLYTHE STREET	MERSEY ST. SENIOR AND JUNIOR	GIRLS' „ „ „
CURRIE JUNIOR	MOUNTCOLLYER	ST. MALACHY'S
DUNCAIRN	MOUNTPOTTINGER	C.B. (OXFORD STREET)
EARL STREET BOYS'	NEW ROAD SENIOR	CONVENT (SUSSEX PLACE)
GIRLS'	JUNIOR	ST. MATTHEW'S BOYS'
INFANTS'	PORTER	GIRLS'
GROVE	QUEEN VICTORIA	ST. PATRICK'S
HILLMAN	ST. ANTHONY'S (MILLFIELD)	BOYS' (DONEGALL STREET)
LANCASTER STREET	BOYS' AND GIRLS'	GIRLS' „ „
LINFIELD SENIOR	ST. BARNABAS	C.B. „ „
JUNIOR	ST. COLMAN'S	ST. PAUL'S (CANNING STREET)
MABEL STREET	ST. COMGALL'S BOYS' AND GIRLS'	SANDY ROW
MAGDALENE	ST. GEORGE'S	SEAMEN'S
MARINERS	ST. JOSEPH'S BOYS' (YORK ROAD)	STRAND
McQUISTON	GIRLS' „ „	TEMPLEMORE AVENUE
		WORKMAN
		YORK STREET

Assembly Instructions for **UNREGISTERED CHILDREN** will be given by Poster outside the Schools named above.

NO OTHER UNREGISTERED PERSONS WILL BE EVACUATED FOR THE PRESENT.

Stormont Castle, Belfast,   July 4th, 1940.

INTRODUCTION

This book is the first time that the story of the Belfast Blitz of April and May 1941 has been told from the perspective of those who lived through the experience. The value of using this eye-witness history, accounts from people who witnessed the events, is that it gives us a real sense of what it meant to live through the Belfast Blitz, a sense of what people saw and experienced and how they felt.

The 150 contributions from nurses, policemen, government officials, journalists, and ordinary civilians that make up this book form a remarkable documentary history of a critical event in the story of twentieth-century Belfast. This is not an 'oral' history in the conventionally understood sense of later reminiscence – much of the material in the book was written in 1941 or very soon thereafter. Instead, the piecing together of these many voices will, I hope, shape for the reader a narrative not mediated by time or later recollection and thus altered in the process. Researching all the available written sources I have constantly been struck by the freshness and honesty of what people had to say and how unsentimentally they recorded the events of 1941.

So what sort of city was Belfast in 1941? In the years leading up to the declaration of war, it was very much a divided place. A series of violent sectarian riots had erupted in July 1935 and had lasted for almost two months. By the time an uneasy peace had returned, thirteen people were dead, scores more were injured and over two thousand Catholics had been driven from their homes.

The strain that this placed on people was palpable, and was compounded by the difficult financial climate. The Depression of the 1930s had hit the city hard. Linen was still the staple trade, easily the biggest employer, but the rates of pay were low and much of the workforce female. As a result, the number of those receiving help from the Poor Law Union (the Workhouse) was on the rise – in 1937 it was 4,967; in 1938 that had risen to 6,326; and in 1939 it had reached 7,183 – and the Guardians (those who supervised the workhouse and collected the Poor Rate), wrote of facing 'sloth, fecklessness and iniquity'.

By the end of the 1930s it was estimated that well over a third of the city was living in absolute poverty, with the housing stock, in particular, little better than slums. Many of the characteristic red-brick, inner-city terraces had been built after 1870 when the city's population exploded, drawing in tens of thousands of people every year from all over Ulster. As the events of April and May 1941 would show, these quickly-thrown-up houses would need relatively little to bring them down.

Bitter social divides, a Corporation permanently short of money, and deeply entrenched sectarian attitudes did little to improve the lives of many of the ordinary citizens whose voices are found in this book.

When the Allies declared war on Germany on 3 September 1939, the feeling in the palatial Parliament Buildings of Stormont was one of sluggish complacency, born of a belief that, initially at least, the geography of Western Europe would protect Northern Ireland from the Luftwaffe. Even when

Germany invaded France in May 1940, occupying all the the territory to the Atlantic coast, and essentially placing Belfast within the reach of a determined enemy, the prevalent belief was that the war wouldn't come to Belfast.

London was an obvious first target for German bombers but in November 1940 their tactics changed and the Luftwaffe concentrated their destructive efforts first on British industrial cities like Coventry, and then on ports and cities that supported the Allied effort in the Battle of the Atlantic. In spite of this, Northern Ireland still felt itself to be relatively secure.

Belfast was actively contributing to the war effort, with shipbuilding firm Harland & Wolff producing aircraft carriers, cruisers (including HMS *Belfast*) and other naval ships, while aircraft manufacturer Short & Harland delivered over one thousand Sterling bombers and 125 Sunderland flying boats, but lack of urgency characterised even their shared efforts. Delivery deadlines were regularly missed and there were frequent strikes; small, though important, examples of the city's complacent attitude.

In spite of having witnessed the devastation wreaked by the Germans on other British cities, Belfast faced 1941 with so few air-raid shelters that, even if all that did exist were fully used, only one quarter of the city's population could be accommodated. And in many other areas baleful under-provision marked the city. Searchlights, barrage balloons and trained staff were all in short supply.

So when the bombs fell that Easter, the resultant level of casualties was high, and little work had been done to provide additional mortuary services. Within days of the raids, St George's Market in the centre of the city and the municipal swimming baths on Belfast's Falls Road had to be used to accommodate corpses recovered from the blitzed areas.

Moya Woodside, one of the most significant chroniclers of the Belfast Blitz.

Historians of this period, especially those concerned with social history, are fortunate that one unusually descriptive diary keeper and chronicler was at work in Belfast from 1940 as part of the Mass Observation Survey, a social research campaign that recruited volunteer dirarists across the United Kingdom. Moya Woodside – MO Diary Number 5462 – is usually described as 'the wife of a Belfast surgeon', but there was a lot more to her than that. Born Moya Neill, she was a member of one of Belfast's most prosperous mercantile families with a long tradition in flour production. Educated at Queen's, she was also an accomplished musician and, between 1937 and 1942, was honorary secretary of the Belfast branch of the Society for Constructive Birth Control, at one stage hosting a visit to the city by Marie Stopes, campaigner for women's rights and pioneer in the field of birth control. In a later memoir she recalled Marie Stopes' presence at a dinner in Belfast – 'Throughout the meal, Dr Stopes ignored the usual social pleasantries, and gave a running lecture on methods of contraception, at one point even producing a Dutch cap from her handbag and passing it round the dinner table … in Belfast, in 1939, such topics were unmentionable in mixed company.'

Woodside's solidly middle-class background, values and social circle coupled with her almost daily contact with the residents of Belfast's slum and working-class districts, make her the most valuable contemporary recorder of Belfast events and attitudes between 1940 and 1942. Her record of the Belfast Blitz and its aftermath is of incalculable value, noting inter alia, panic and evacuation, the needs of refugees, poverty and deprivation especially in housing, damage inflicted on buildings and districts of the city, and the attitudes of middle and upper classes to the endemic deprivation. Importantly, her observations often contrast with the official story circulated by the government at the time.

Of similar social background to Moya Woodside was Emma Duffin, whose father, Adam, was a wealthy Belfast stockbroker, and later a Stormont MP. In World War One she and three of her sisters were members of the Voluntary Aid Detachment, formed by the British Red Cross and the St John Ambulance Society to provide field nursing support. She had worked as a nurse in France from 1916 to 1919 and later was Secretary to the Belfast Council of Social Work. In 1940 she returned to the Voluntary Aid Detachment, this time as Commandant of Stranmillis Military Hospital, a post she served in until she was demobbed in 1943. She died in 1979.

Perhaps the most valuable external perspective on the destruction and chaos in Belfast in the immediate aftermath of both Blitz raids comes from the official reports prepared for the Dublin Government by Major Seán O'Sullivan. He had joined the Irish Army in 1922 and was commissioned as an officer on 1 Oct 1924. His talent was spotted early and two years later he was appointed to the Adjutant General's department. In 1938 he was promoted to Director, Chemical Warfare, and Officer-in-Charge, Air Raid Precautions, and it was in that capacity that he made his two visits to Belfast in the aftermath of the April and May raids. His military eye and politically savvy assessments of the personnel he met in Belfast read today like an insider's account of a city struggling to cope in the hours after the bombs fell. O'Sullivan was later appointed Colonel and served as Senior ADC to President Seán T. Ó Ceallaigh from 1945 until the latter's retirement in 1959.

One other outsider worth mentioning is Doreen Bates – MO Diary Number 5245 – a female tax inspector from suburban London who came to work temporarily in Belfast in March 1941. Her initial observations, committed to her daily diary, can still surprise: 'Belfast is a hideous place. I go the office on a really old tram (for 1d) along streets without one building worth looking at – except perhaps the new BBC building.' There's a lucidity and immediacy to her observations that read like the transcript of a modern radio report: 'Several times the bed swayed like a cot being rocked; doors and windows rattled; shrapnel patted on the shed roof outside; I could see against the blackout the glare of the fires. The most nerve-wracking thing to me was when the Germans glided in silently and the only sound was the crump of bombs.'

The Belfast Blitz remains strong in the folk memory of all parts of the city. More lives were lost in Belfast in a single night – the raid of 15 April – than in any other British city. The random deaths of individuals and entire families, the noise, the fires, the loss of many key buildings, the very reshaping of the city centre were not easily forgotten, nor easily spoken of. *The Belfast Blitz: The People's Story* is a tribute to all those who lived and died during this key moment in Northern Ireland's history, and a testament to those people whose voices and stories are part of this book.

IF THE INVADER COMES
ADVICE TO CIVILIANS
KEEP CALM AND STAY PUT

Don't leave your own area.

Stay in your own home unless you are officially ordered to move.

Take orders only from the Military, the Police, or other authorised persons you know.

Disregard any Instructions you may receive by telephone until you have checked them.

IGNORE RUMOURS. They are probably spread by the enemy.

27th July, 1940.

Issued by the Ministry of Public Security, Northern Ireland.

When I began researching this project, I made a decision not to standardise or modernise the extracts unless it was necessary for clarity. As much as possible, I have retained the original spelling and grammar so as to preserve the voices of the contributors. Any additional information that has been included appears in square brackets and, occasionally, in a footnote.

Where extracts were dated, such as those taken from diaries and letters, I have included the date in the extract. I have not, however, felt the need to include dates for all the extracts since this is usually evident from the content and from the events being described.

Before the
Bombs

The period between the German invasion of Poland on 1 September 1939 and the subsequent invasions of countries such as France, Luxembourg and the Netherlands in the spring of 1940 was a relatively tranquil time for most of the United Kingdom, and Belfast was no different. The war was taking place elsewhere: those residents who cared to follow events in continental Europe did so as bystanders.

After the Nazi sweep into France and the humiliation of Dunkirk, the Northern Ireland government belatedly recognised the need to prepare for war. In June 1940 Major John MacDermott, an eminent pre-war QC, was appointed Stormont Minister of Public Security. Selected for his organising genius, he was charged with ramping up the defences of Northern Ireland. However, one of his first attempts to galvanise Belfast – the evacuation to the country of primary-school children – ended in failure, with a take-up rate of barely ten per cent.

MacDermott's cabinet colleagues had had to sacrifice a portion of their salary to pay for the new minister and their ensuing vigilance over public expenditure hampered his efforts to provide adequately for Belfast's defences. But money was only part of the problem. The other was the near total inability of his colleagues to appreciate how ruthless the

Germans were likely to be. Rather than build many thousands of air-raid shelters, he opted instead for large public shelters in the city centre, though as historian Jonathan Bardon during a lecture given at the War Memorial Lecture Building in April 2010 pointed out, 'by the beginning of 1941 there were only four public air-raid shelters made of sandbags round the City Hall, together with underground toilets at Shaftesbury Square and Donegall Square North ... The city had no fighter squadrons, no balloon barrage and only 21 anti-aircraft guns when the war began, and only around 2,000 civil defence volunteers had been trained.'

At the end of November 1940 members of a Luftwaffe reconnaissance mission took photographs of the city's main industrial and military targets, including Victoria Barracks, Harland & Wolff, Short & Harland, the Gasworks and Belfast Power Station. But it was clear that the entire city of Belfast, including all its residential and commercial areas, would make a good target for a future air raid. It was virtually undefended.

The Germans changed their tactics in the spring of 1941 and – in an attempt to destroy the wider war economy – increased the number of cities they planned to attack. The first German attack on Belfast occurred on the night of 7/8 April 1941 when a number of bombers, perhaps as few as six, split from a main raid on the critical shipbuilding facilities on Clydeside to drop bombs on east Belfast. As a result of their accurate targeting, the small number of bombers caused considerable damage to the McCue Dick timber yard in Duncrue Street, Harland & Wolff, and to the inner-city community of Ballymacarrett. The illusion that Belfast could never, and would never, be a target was gone.

One soldier who recorded this first raid on Belfast was a decorated chaplain, the Reverend J.E.G. Quinn, on leave in

Belfast with his parents. He had already won the Military Cross for bravery at Dunkirk. His diary records an Easter weekend of fine weather and – even after the 7/8 April raid – the relaxed atmosphere in the city. On Easter Monday evening, as he sailed to England just twenty-four hours before the Luftwaffe arrived en masse, he noted, 'Belfast looked lovely as we left it under the stars.'

IDENTITY CARDS

1

YOU MUST NOW COMPLETE YOUR IDENTITY CARD BY ENTERING YOUR USUAL ADDRESS, SIGNATURE AND DATE IN THE SPACES PROVIDED. The Cards of children under 14 must be signed and taken care of by the parent or other person in charge, instead of by the child. The child's age or date of birth must be written under the child's name in upper right-hand portion of Card.

2

IF YOUR IDENTITY CARD IS LOST, DESTROYED OR BADLY DEFACED, a new one must be obtained at once from your National Registration Office, which is located at the Food Office. If you subsequently find the lost Card it must be handed in immediately to that Office. ANY CARD IN YOUR POSSESSION relating to a person who is dead, or has joined the Army, or has gone away without leaving an address, MUST ALSO BE HANDED IN. If you find a lost Identity Card you must at once take it to a Police Station or National Registration Office: a reward will be paid.

3

IF YOU REMOVE TO A NEW PERMANENT ADDRESS you must call within seven days at the National Registration Office (Food Office) in the new locality and notify the removal, producing your Identity Card for official correction. This is not necessary for a temporary absence on business or holidays, PROVIDED THAT YOUR TEMPORARY ADDRESS IS KNOWN AT YOUR HOME and can be obtained there by the authorities.

4
IT IS A PUNISHABLE OFFENCE

(a) to keep AN IDENTITY CARD OTHER THAN YOUR OWN, unless you are in charge of the person to whom it relates;
(b) to keep TWO IDENTITY CARDS relating to the same person;
(c) to keep an Identity Card containing particulars which you KNOW TO BE INCORRECT;
(d) to allow ANY UNAUTHORISED PERSON TO HAVE POSSESSION of your Identity Card;
(e) to fail to GIVE NOTICE OF REMOVAL, or to neglect to arrange that any temporary address of yours can be ASCERTAINED AT YOUR USUAL RESIDENCE.

PERSONS OVER FOURTEEN SHOULD ALWAYS CARRY THEIR IDENTITY CARDS. THEY MUST BE SHOWN ON DEMAND TO POLICE CONSTABLES IN UNIFORM OR SOLDIERS ON DUTY.

Further information can be obtained at any Food and National Registration Office in Northern Ireland.

ISSUED BY THE REGISTRAR-GENERAL, NORTHERN IRELAND.

BELFAST NEWS LETTER

6

Moya Woodside
Elmwood Avenue, south Belfast
7 March 1940

After reading a letter in the *Manchester Guardian*, describing the horrors experienced by the Jewish people transported from Soviet Poland to labour camps in the Ural mountains, I feel ashamed and smitten of my petty complaints and discontent with my own comfortable existence.

Here in Ireland is probably the pleasantest place in Europe at the present time – we are unbombed, we have no conscription, there is still plenty to eat, life is reasonably normal. Sufferings such as those described in the letter – of hunger, disease, separation, appalling conditions and inhumanity – are unknown to anyone, in fact, they are inconceivable. Yet for the greater part of the time one is conscious of positive inconveniences or drawbacks, and only remembers intermittently and with a sense of guilt the negative blessings – the things which are not happening.

Captain M.J. Pleydell
206 Field Ambulance, Lisburn
5 August 1940

In the evening, two of us went up to Lough Neagh. It was lovely there, peace and quiet. Just the lapping of the waves on the shore, and the fishermen had their nets drying in the sun. There were purple mountains standing out far beyond the Lough, and the fishermen were talking away.

Then a motorboat came chugging across from nowhere and the noise of its engine seemed very strange. The men steered her with oars across the shallow water.

'Och yes,' they said, 'it's funny to think we're at war.'

'And Hitler is a troublesome bhoy,' said another.
And so we left them and drove back to Belfast.

Moya Woodside
Elmwood Avenue, south Belfast
15 August 1940

Arrival of 'Stay Where You Are Leaflet' which seems better
worded and more to the point than previous efforts. I doubt
though if mere words and exhortations will be enough to
conquer panic if, and when, invasion occurs.

The local press reports an improved response to the second
Belfast evacuation scheme, the first having been a complete
flop with less than ten per cent even registering.

The construction of air raid shelters at the end of the
avenue continues apace, but from their position it is obvious
that there will be many traffic accidents during the winter
black-out. My maid comments on the openings to the shelter,
and says it is a good thing they face towards the centre of the
avenue, as otherwise coming home at night after dark she
might expect to be pulled inside off the pavement and
embraced. It seems the shelters are now very popular for
courting couples, as well as providing opportunities for ill-
disposed men.

20 August 1940

At the pictures last night. The 'Universal' newsreel was too
stale and boring for words – nine items out of a total of ten
showed military on ARP [Air Raid Precautions] activities, all
accompanied by facetious commentary. It was received in
apathetic silence except for the customary claps when King
and Queen appeared. The whole effect was of complete
unreality, where everyone in the audience knew that air raids

Issued by the Ministry of   Information on behalf of
the War Office and the Ministry of Home Security

STAY WHERE YOU ARE

IF this island is invaded by sea or air everyone who is not under orders must stay where he or she is. This is not simply advice : it is an order from the Government, and you must obey it just as soldiers obey their orders. Your order is " Stay Put ", but remember that this does not apply until invasion comes.

Why must I stay put?

Because in France, Holland and Belgium, the Germans were helped by the people who took flight before them. Great crowds of refugees blocked all roads. The soldiers who could have defended them could not get at the enemy. The enemy used the refugees as a human shield. These refugees were got out on to the roads by rumour and false orders. Do not be caught out in this way. Do not take any notice of any story telling what the enemy has done or where he is. Do not take orders except from the Military, the Police, the Home Guard (L.D.V.) and the A.R.P. authorities or wardens.

What will happen to me if I don't stay put?

If you do not stay put you will stand a very good chance of being killed. The enemy may machine-gun you from the air in order to increase panic, or you may run into enemy forces which have landed behind you. An official German message was captured in Belgium which ran :

" Watch for civilian refugees on the roads. Harass them as much as possible."

Our soldiers will be hurrying to drive back the invader and will not be able to stop and help you. On the contrary, they will are of daily occurrence and creating havoc in the usual routine of life, yet they were not so much as mentioned. Compare with this week's issue of *Picture Post* which has pages of photographs taken before, during and after an actual raid. Both interesting and instructive. I feel that this cautious film censorship is psychologically wrong. People are less liable to panic if they are told the truth in a reasonable manner and know what to expect.

G.T. Harris
RAF Coastal Command, Newtownards
29 August 1940

One hardly knows what to do with one's time at Newtownards. There is nothing to do all day and little by night. True there are two picture houses and Belfast is only nine miles away. But films do not have much attention for me nowadays, while Belfast has little to offer except crowds of people which makes one desire to shed one's uniform, once and for all. I am counting the days as they pass. Another three weeks and I shall be home and on leave. I wonder if England has been bombed much?

31 August 1940

Stung by the bombing of Berlin, Hitler renews his aerial attacks on a large scale. The fighter command breaks up the assault, shooting down eighty and ninety planes. In Ireland we find ourselves in the fortunate position of being spectators. I wonder how long this state of affairs will last? Belfast will make a good target. You can't miss it. And they don't trouble about blackout much in Northern Ireland.

18 October 1940

Newtownards is a quiet peaceful place these war days. So is all of Northern Ireland for that matter. The chief topic in the correspondence columns is the speed of military vehicles, which is claimed to be excessive, and the fact that Ulster is not making enough money out of the war. These horrors claim quite a lot of attention.

I, for my part, would like Belfast shook up by a good heavy aerial bombardment.

Fred Bashford
Headquarters, British Troops Northern Ireland,
Belvoir Park, south Belfast
23 October 1940

Belfast is still dreaming pretty successfully of the idyllic days of peace: there seems to be no more than a smudge of the war-stain on her countenance yet.

23 December 1940

Things are very quiet down here. Nothing ever stirs except the wind bringing faint echoes of a war being fought with a vain savagery at London, Coventry, Sheffield – or the bitter sands of Libya.

Except for an unidentified plane which brought half-a-dozen shots from AA [anti-aircraft] guns one night, Ireland has not yet broken peace with the world, which is rather remarkable when one considers all the blood and grief that have drenched the green land through the years.

Moya Woodside
Elmwood Avenue, south Belfast
2 January 1941

All of a sudden everybody seems to have become incendiary-bomb conscious, whether it be the result of local propaganda

MINISTRY OF PUBLIC SECURITY
PROTECTION AGAINST
HIGH EXPLOSIVE BOMBS

A vital responsibility lies on each Householder to ensure that adequate shelter is available for himself and his dependants.

HAVE YOU ADAPTED SOME PART OF YOUR HOUSE AS A REFUGE?

There should be rules for each family to follow if there is an air raid.

DO THE MEMBERS OF YOUR FAMILY KNOW WHAT TO DO?

There are certain things which might be needed in a shelter—respirators, first-aid outfit, a torch or candle, drinking water.

SEE TO THESE THINGS NOW.

An Article on Page 3 gives some advice about shelters. If you want help, ask your nearest Warden.

MINISTRY OF PUBLIC SECURITY
PRECAUTIONS AGAINST
INCENDIARY BOMBS

CLEAR YOUR ROOF SPACES AND ATTICS OF ANY OLD JUNK COLLECTED THERE, AND SEE THAT YOU CAN EASILY GET INTO THE ROOF SPACE.

HAVE READY AS MANY BUCKETS AS POSSIBLE, A SHOVEL OR SCOOP, PREFERABLY WITH A LONG HANDLE, AND SOME SAND OR DRY EARTH.

IF POSSIBLE PROVIDE A STIRRUP PUMP, FAILING THIS A GARDEN SYRINGE IS USEFUL, OR OLD BLANKETS SOAKED IN WATER. KEEP YOUR BATH FILLED WITH WATER.

TRY TO TACKLE AN INCENDIARY BOMB YOURSELF IF ONE FALLS ON YOUR HOUSE. SEE PAGE 3, WHERE AN ARTICLE GIVES INSTRUCTIONS HOW TO DO THIS.

or the recent raid on the city [the London Blitz of 29 December 1940]. The papers are full of what to do and how to do it (it is all made to sound as easy as playing with bucket and spade at the seaside); the head of this household spent yesterday afternoon running up and down to the attic with sandbags and so on; my maid returning from her day off said she found her father very agitated and making similar preparations.

9 January 1941

We had an 'alert' at lunchtime today. The sky was clear and sun shining, so it was obvious that no vast force of enemy raiders could be approaching, but nevertheless, watching at the window, I could see our warden rushing aimlessly up and down the street, clad in heavy mackintosh, tin hat, gas mask and other paraphernalia. (This man is an elderly retired police inspector, cordially loathed in the district for his officiousness.) We sat down to lunch and soon there was a loud knock at the door.

My maid answered, there were sounds of argument, and then she came into the dining room and said we were ordered to put out a bucket of water during an alert and this was the only house which hadn't done so, so HE says scornfully. 'It was the first I had heard of such a regulation. What use would a couple of buckets of water be in an air raid anyway?'

By the time the maid had reluctantly fetched a bucket the All Clear had started sounding. She said to me afterwards, 'People aren't allowed private lives anymore. It's nothing but muddling and interference from old fuss pots like HIM, with nothing else to do.'

26 January 1941

Coming home again reflected on the dismal appearance of

downtown streets on Sunday. Nothing, not even a café open, and nowhere for people to go.

A crowd of men from the shipyards get on the tram, tired and dirty; and I wondered just how much longer people would stand for the hypocrisy of clergy and city fathers, who fly into a frenzy of Sabbatarianism when anyone suggests opening the cinemas on Sundays, yet who don't ... actively oppose these working men who sweat a seven-day week to help ensure their safety.

5 February 1941

A woman in the slums told me this morning that before she left Birmingham 'one o them insanitary bombs' had fallen on her house. Visited another bombed out family, also back from Birmingham, who are now living (five people) in two minute and dilapidated rooms for which they pay eight shillings rent.

They are awaiting £50 compensation for their old house and in the meantime have literally only what they stand up in, bedclothes, whatever, some makeshift furniture, and a borrowed saucepan. The man's job has gone too, from earning £4.15 a week they are reduced to Unemployment Benefit. *And nobody cares.* War affects everyone but as usual the very poor are the worst sufferers.

6 February 1941

A young barrister friend, Catholic, who is frequently in Éire and knows many influential personages there, says there is a large body of opinion which hates the British and especially Churchill and which would prefer a German invasion, and if necessary, occupation rather than have English troops back again. Churchill's speech about the ports was considered tactless in the extreme.

Should an invasion actually occur, it is doubtful if the help even then of the British would be welcomed. Past history has always mattered more to Irish nationalists than the actual present.

14 February 1941

Notice that the wife of the recently appointed Minister of Public Security has herself been appointed head organiser for the local WVS* and that Dr Little, member for Co. Down, has been complaining in Parliament that the supply of gold braid for naval officers in Ulster is insufficient, will the government please do something about it? Ulster is certainly a wonderful place to live in.

Doreen Bates
Tax Inspector
Sydenham, east Belfast
8 March 1941

Belfast is a hideous place. I go to the office on a really old tram (for 1d) along streets without one building worth looking at – except perhaps the new BBC building. It still surprises to see unbroken windows.

There are plenty of surface shelters and a few balloons** to protect Harland and Wolff shipbuilding yards. At the office there is a serious fire-watching scheme and all the windows

---

* Women's Voluntary Service which, in addition to some Civil Defence duties, organised rest centres providing meals and washing facilities for those left homeless after a raid.

** Barrage balloons played an important part in the defence of key military and industrial sites. Best understood as large air ships tethered to the ground by steel cables, they had one principal purpose – to deny low-level airspace to the Luftwaffe.

are covered with paper criss-crossed. It has been blowing a gale, pouring with rain and very cold.

I could not face hunting for somewhere to live and buried my gloom in a cinema – two American films, neither good, but it was a distraction. It is now 9.45 p.m. and I shall go to bed and read.

Minute Book, Principal Teachers' Union
8 March 1941

After some discussion on fire watching the following resolution was passed on the motion of Mr MacCartney, seconded by Miss Robertson – 'While teachers are willing, and indeed anxious, to take part in essential services during the present international crisis, the members of the Principal Teachers' Union most emphatically protest against asking women teachers to volunteer for fire watching in schools at night.'

Doreen Bates
Tax Inspector
Sydenham, east Belfast
9 March 1941

On the whole I have got through today (Sunday) better than I expected. I had breakfast at 9.15 and read all morning. Ordered papers … and was mildly surprised to be able to get a *Telegraph* (though in the afternoon) and the *Sunday Times* (though not till midday). It made me feel more at home to read it as normal but more thoroughly. After lunch I wrote some letters and went out. I found two small parks, saw the university and the river Lagan and another route to the centre.

I detect some ill-feeling between the old lady party and the 'services' party. But the most interesting thing was the general dislike of Priestley's postscript* – general but stronger among the 'army' wives.

They complain that he is boring, dictatorial and unpatriotic and ask how his wife can bear to be with him. He evidently makes them uncomfortable and I suspect because he gets under their skin. This war will have achieved some good if it manages even a little to shake up the people who live in this hotel.

11 March 1941

Two possibilities for living here have emerged. H. knows a woman with two little girls, husband in the Admiralty, who takes paying guests at Holywood, the suburb where he lives. She had two houses in London but they have been bombed and she wants to make a little money to substitute.

The other is a furnished flat at £2.2 per week at Sydenham, a slightly nearer suburb. The flat attracts me because of the independence but it would probably be more expensive. The shops aren't bad, there are fascinating tweeds – more stockings than in England, but expensive. There is a monster Woolworth's, all its counters loaded, a contrast from the last few branches I saw in and around London with half tier counters being used.

The typist approves of me and wishes I were permanently at Belfast. She told me there was a lot of feeling against England and the war in Belfast [and that people would]

---

* J.B. Priestley, the novelist and playwright, delivered a regular Sunday evening postscript on BBC radio throughout much of 1940 and 1941. His success as a wartime radio broadcaster is widely attributed to his ability to articulate the shared experiences and similar feelings of his listeners. When he was dropped by the BBC it was believed to be because of his overt left-wing sympathies.

'just as soon live under Hitler' but it is less openly said now.

16 March 1941

After breakfast I set out for a walk on the hill you can see from all over the town. Not having a map I just walked straight for it from the hotel. First through small squalid houses and across a dismal bog with an engineering works on it. Hundreds of small children – some pretty, not stupid looking and all dirty were playing in the streets. I counted eighty-two in two minutes. I have never seen so many tramps in such a small area.

On blank walls were scrawled IRA slogans: *England's difficulty is Ireland's opportunity – Men, the IRA call you – You can break our bodies, not our spirits – Up the IRA*, even some chalked swastikas. Then across the Falls Rd, an interminable road by the cemetery – allotments – last gaps of hedges and the houses were left behind. I was climbing all the way for the bog till I reached a wide path.

21 March 1941

The night before last, London had its heaviest raid since the city fire, the first serious raid since I left. I didn't really get worked up till the evening and then the news fixed my mind on it and I couldn't keep my thoughts off E. and the family, I felt desperate, so helpless in the complete silence here, infinitely worse than I have felt on any occasion in London.

Reverend Dr James Little MP*
Westminster MP for County Down
1 April 1941

I want to say that the electors who have sent the representatives of Northern Ireland to this House are most determined and uncompromising in their opposition to this proposed Regulation for the opening of theatres and music-halls on Sundays, as they feel that what is being attempted in England to-day will be attempted in Ulster to-morrow, and this degradation of the Lord's Day our people in Ulster will not have at any cost.

In the days of Queen Victoria, of blessed memory, no business of any kind was transacted upon a Sunday that could be transacted on another day of the week. To-day, to our hurt and loss, we have gone to the other extreme and anything that can well be done on a week-day must be done on a Sunday.

I have noticed that at these Sunday entertainments there has been only a small number of soldiers present. I am satisfied that the demand for Sunday theatres and music-halls arises far more from a desire for gain than from any altruistic desire to entertain our soldiers.

There has been a repeated demand for the opening of cinemas in Belfast on Sunday, on the plea that the military wanted such opening, but no soldier has ever said to me that he wanted to attend any such show. The people of Northern Ireland treat the soldiers with every kindness, and the men themselves would seem to prefer a quiet Sunday evening in a home or hall, in Christian surroundings, to any show or entertainment.

---

* Taken from a House of Commons debate on Emergency Powers (Defence) Acts, where he identified potential non-observation of the Sabbath as a major change in Northern Ireland life.

Belfast News Letter
8 April 1941

The following official statement was issued this morning by the Ministry of Public Security, Northern Ireland: 'A small force of enemy bombers, one of which was shot down over the sea by our night fighters and blew up in mid-air, attacked an area in Northern Ireland and caused some damage to industrial, commercial and other property. Some casualties were unfortunately caused. Further details will be issued later in the day.'

A *News Letter* reporter states that a church was hit, and also houses in a working class area. Several people received slight injuries from falling shrapnel.

The anti-aircraft gunfire continued intermittent for several hours. Windows in many houses were shattered.

HOW RAIDER WAS BROUGHT DOWN

Describing how a German aircraft was brought down during Monday night's raid on Northern Ireland, the Air Ministry News Service says:—

"A Hurricane squadron leader patrolling the coast of Northern Ireland sighted two raiders. He closed on the rear one, silenced the gunner with his second burst, and saw the raider blow up after the third burst."

BELFAST NEWS LETTER

Moya Woodside
Elmwood Avenue, south Belfast
8 April 1941

Belfast had its first raid last night – and I would not believe it was on! I was just falling asleep when I heard thumps and lumps and a loud bang, followed by the sirens. My husband came in and said 'They're dropping bombs, better come down to the kitchen.' We have had so many false alarms that, in my drowsy state, I muttered something about it being only anti-aircraft fire, and stayed where I was. Banging and distant thumping continued, for all the world like a magnificent Guy Fawkes celebration. I could not hear any planes, and came to the conclusion that the din was just some form of 'practice'. There was a silence, broken by the ringing of the telephone. (This may have been about 1.00 a.m.) I heard my husband hurriedly dressing, and rushing out of the house with great slamming of doors.

The barrage soon started again but I tried to pay no attention to it, nor to the vague noises which were going on, and I have a faint recollection of the All Clear sounding just before I finally succeeded in getting to sleep again.

This morning I was astonished to hear from my husband that there had been a genuine raid, and that he had been called to the hospital as additional staff to help the large numbers of injured. 'They got _____, _____ and _____ ' he said, mentioning a number of places near the docks. We only live about one and a half miles from there; it seems amazing that all this can have happened so near, while I lay calmly in bed (and I am not by any means deaf!).

Later

Sole topic of conversation is last night's raid. Streets, shops, trams, phone calls, even perfect strangers are talking about it.

Everyone anxious to recount their reactions/experiences and to cap the other fellow's story of damage done. In the library I heard an elderly woman retelling at great length the behaviour of her dog. At monthly Clinic committee a row of haggard faces were assembled, and I was surprised to hear that I was unique in having spent the entire night in bed, and in ignorance. Several women, living much further out of town, had spent the night in shelters, while others had stayed up watching the fires, and one had even gone for a walk at 4.00 a.m. on the nearby hills to get a better view. Two friends of mine who occupy a top bedroom in a boarding house said the entire population of the house (nine women, one man) spent the raid in their bedroom, watching the illuminations in an atmosphere of hysteria. I suggested they lock their door next time!

Doreen Bates
Tax Inspector
Sydenham, east Belfast
8 April 1941

Last night I heard the siren again … had just fallen asleep when gunfire awoke me and few minutes later the sirens went. I considered and decided there was no point in getting up. There are two bay windows in my ground floor bedroom but the bed is in the far corner. I heard the Bennetts above me getting up and she was excited. I hadn't heard the planes come over. She reported that there was a big fire (which I heard today was a timber yard.) The AA [anti-aircraft] sounded very poppety and shallow after the heavy London barrage. The earlier planes kept high but later they evidently found that the AA was not much risk and they flew lower.

There were long intervals when I must have slept but several times bombs and planes and gunfire awoke me. They dropped three landmines – two fell in the Lough but one hit a spare parts factory and killed workmen rumoured to number from six to one hundred. The alert was 12.15 – 04.15. One plane was brought down by a fighter near Larne, exploded in the air.

I could hear people running about the road and also the patter of shrapnel and popping of machine guns. There was much excitement this morning. Miss H, my typist who lives with her people near the river over their shop, said their shop window was blown in.

I was not as jittery as I was after the heavy London raid last month worrying about people, but it is worse here than at Purley because it is a smaller place. One feels more conscious and more part of the target all the time.

Holy Family Parish Chronicle
Newington Avenue, north Belfast
8 April 1941

The sirens sounded and the first air raid took place in the city. A high explosive fell in Alexandra Park Avenue in this parish and also in Alexander Park but there were no casualties in this parish – a few houses were wrecked but no Catholic houses suffered.

J.C. Beckett
Lisburn, County Antrim
8 April 1941

We retired rather before midnight. Before I had gone to sleep I heard an explosion (AA [anti-aircraft] gun, I thought). It was 12.10. Five minutes later sirens and explosions began

BELFAST INFIRMARY

WANTED
VOLUNTEERS FOR FIRE FIGHTING
and STRETCHER BEARING DUTIES

THE COMMISSIONERS OF THE Belfast Union make an urgent appeal for VOLUNTEERS for FIRE FIGHTING and STRETCHER BEAR-ING duties at the Belfast Infirmary.

Compensation to Enrolled Volunteers against injury in the performance of these duties is covered by Act of Parliament.

Names and addresses to be furnished to the undersigned.

(Signed) R. W. CRAIG,
Clerk of Union.
Clerk's Office, 51, Lisburn Road,
Belfast. Telephone 20861.
Dated this 8th day of April, 1941.

almost simultaneously, and our first raid was in full swing. It was 4.30 before I got back to bed. On the whole I enjoyed it, though at times it was boring enough.

We had quite a good view of the main fire, and the explosions were near enough to be exciting. The house shook, doors and windows rattled, and more than once we expected one of the windows to crash in. I had W.G. Bennett and Ted McManus with me, and on the whole I think they enjoyed it quite as much as I did.

Sir Wilfrid Spender
Head of the Northern Ireland Civil Service
Stormont, east Belfast
8 April 1941

The enemy attacked Belfast last night in broad moonlight making a series of attacks with probably five different bombers.

The bombing seems unfortunately to have been very accurate in causing serious damage in an important part of Harland and Wolff as well as on to other buildings in the docks area and adjacent residential quarters. A good many casualties were caused and I fear that one important branch of Harland and Wolff's works may be thrown out of gear for some time.

The full moon is on the 11th inst and therefore an attack during the next nine days must be anticipated. I thought the barrage of our guns sounded very slight compared with the barrage of the last war and was rather surprised that I heard the plane before the guns, and the guns before the 'alert'.

Moya Woodside
Elmwood Avenue, south Belfast
9 April 1941

Air raid still monopolises conversation. Everyone has, or claims to have, a different 'inside' story of the damage done. Panic seems to have been widespread though the damage done was actually on a very small scale, confined in truth to 'military objectives'. Other damage was apparently incidental. The result goes to prove, in many people's opinion, that the blackout, at least on a moonlit night, is just a waste of time. Last few nights the town must have been spread out to the airman's view as in a photograph.

Local newspaper reports said, almost as if it occurred in Timbuktu, 'some damage to houses'; interview with rector of bombed church (unidentified), write-ups of heroism in dealing with incendiaries etc. No suggestion anywhere that anything of importance was hit, or that anyone was unpleasantly wounded.

Having myself access to 'inside' information via the hospital and with relatives of two men working in the 'military objective', I am able to assess something of the inadequacy of the official and press reports. It makes one wonder just how much *isn't being told* all over England and Scotland when for once we know the truth ourselves.

I suppose it is 'keeping up morale' for the general public to be lulled in ignorance, and for them not to know about men with both legs blown off, backs broken, half their faces gone – or worse.

Doreen Bates
Tax Inspector
Sydenham, east Belfast
11 April 1941

Two days gap because I have left the diary till after the news and then lingered talking to the Bennetts till my fire was out. First some footnotes to Monday's raid. Casualties were eight killed, two missing – the rumours soared to one hundred and fifty.

Almost all were in the one factory on night shift. I hear that an unexploded shell came through the roof of a house across the road, through the ceiling, and made a mess of the bedroom. The people had just gone downstairs. We now have a smoke screen on moonlit nights when the weather is suitable. Mrs B thought it was poison gas the first night.

We have had instructions about what to do if the office is damaged. I have called at the blood transfusion service and transferred here from London.

Moya Woodside
Elmwood Avenue, south Belfast
11 April 1941

It would seem there are three main types of reaction to raids.

Those whose whole life seems conditioned by the possibility of a raid; who are constantly thinking about it; constantly unable to sleep or sleep badly; won't go out in the evenings; run around at night filling baths and buckets and turning off taps etc; talking about the certainty of more and worse raids, with a sort of eager gloom.

Those who do not bother with raids or precautions in the daytime; but who become hysterical and lose their nerve (and indeed their commonsense) if a raid actually occurs.

Those who adopt a fatalistic attitude to the whole thing; who take no precautions and remain calm, resolutely quelling what imagination they possess.

14 April 1941 (Easter Monday)

Shops still closed; genial atmosphere of holiday. Went with friends to suburban picture house in the afternoon, and were stopped at the entrance by a policeman demanding identity cards. We said 'what for' and he said 'I've orders' but on being jokingly further pressed he said that a bomb might fall on the picture house and it would be difficult sorting bodies out afterwards if they had no identifications and anyway 'it was orders'. Rather a macabre preliminary to our afternoon's pleasure.

Lady Lilian Spender
Stormont, east Belfast
14 April 1941

Monday being a holiday for Wolf [sic], and we being well off for petrol as the car had been laid up for so long, decided to have a real treat, and took lunch down to Mahee Island, and had a good walk. A lovely day between the heavy showers and Strangford Lough looking its best.

The joy of being in the country again and smelling the sea. We had to lunch in the car owing to a shower at the wrong moment, and afterwards Wolf and I went for a stroll over the Nendrum ruins, and just as we were looking down at the peaceful little bay behind the Abbey, we heard firing, and realised a raid must be on, so hurried back to Comber but when we got there, the All Clear had sounded, and it proved to have been only one raider.

Belfast News Letter
15 April 1941

Enemy aircraft were active over various parts of the United Kingdom, including Ulster in daylight yesterday. The following joint communiqué was issued by the Northern Ireland Ministry of Public Security and RAF Headquarters yesterday afternoon: 'Enemy aircraft were over Northern Ireland this afternoon. No damage or casualties have so far been reported.'

At one place guns were in action twice, and an enemy aircraft was seen flying at a great height and the noise of fighter machines was believed to have been heard behind the clouds.

Hundreds of people on holiday were in the streets at the time and many of them made their way to shelters. Within a few minutes the thoroughfares were cleared.

Nellie Bell (née Gordon)
Married to Bob Bell on Easter Monday, 1941
Crosscollyer Street, north Belfast

So here we were in Sinclair Seaman's Church at 1.30 p.m. There was quite a crowd in church, lots of friends of his and

Bob and Nellie Bell on their wedding day, 14 April 1941

mine and of course our relations as well. Just as we were married and signing the register the air raid sirens wailed and being down at the docks (a target area) we were all scared; so when we came out to walk down the church to duck the showers of confetti, we found very few people about, a few friends and of course our relations and we did have to duck and we stood about while our Jim took the photographs.

I can't remember being very scared but I was worried about the state some of our relations were in, for some were country folk and were worried about being in Belfast never mind in an air raid. Actually we had had no really bad experiences ourselves up to this point.

Well off we all went to the Carlton Hotel for the reception in Donegall Place it was. It was not usual for people like us to have a reception at all, but it was agreed for us to have this as I had nobody to help me to have it at home. My mother was dead about four years and I had been keeping the home together since that time and I just couldn't have done it for I was working full-time in Gallaher's.

Just as the meal started the All Clear went and we were all so relieved. We didn't know then that the planes overhead were reconnaissance planes and that next night the real thing was to happen.

Easter Tuesday
Raid

Physical damage caused by the raid of 7/8 April was confined largely to the docks area and while there were fatalities – thirteen people died – this raid was only a curtain-raiser. Government officials ordered additional searchlights and anti-aircraft batteries from Britain but for most Belfast residents, in the run-up to the Easter weekend, it was the prospect of the holidays that was the main preoccupation.

Then, as now, Easter Monday and Tuesday (which fell on 14 and 15 April in 1941), were observed as holidays in Northern Ireland, and while Belfast was not exactly en fête, shops were closed, football matches were played and the nearby coastal towns of Bangor, Donaghadee and Whitehead were busy.

Little heed was paid to the single German reconnaissance aircraft over Belfast that Easter Monday, but those who heard and saw the plane didn't forget it. The next afternoon another German plane was spotted, especially by many attending the Linfield versus Distillery match at Windsor Park.

That evening in north-west France, German air crews, numbering almost two hundred, climbed into their planes to begin the thousand-mile journey to Belfast where their targets would be key industrial sites in the harbour area. Using radio beacons for guidance, the bombers flew north over Cherbourg to Cardigan Bay on the Welsh coast and then further north to a point off the County Down coast near Ardglass.

In Belfast, the air-raid sirens began to sound at 22.40. Fifty minutes later the first groups of bombers flew over Belfast Lough, illuminated by vivid moonlight.

The Belfast Blitz had begun in earnest.

Nellie Bell (née Gordon),
Married to Bob Bell on Easter Monday, 1941
Crosscollyer Street, north Belfast

It was arranged that Bob and me would please ourselves what to do Easter Tuesday but we would go for our tea to Bobbie's. I think we just wandered about town and I have a notion we went to Bangor for the afternoon, I'm not quite sure. The trauma afterwards put lots of things out of our minds. Anyhow we left Bobbie's and Maisie's around 10.30 or so in Hatfield St and we got tram to the City Hall. We could have got any one of about four trams which would have taken us home from there. We were in Donegall Place when the sirens went at 11.15 or so. We hopped on to a Midland Railway tram and jumped off and got home as quickly as possible …

My father was sitting in his slippers by the fire. He had had a few drinks but was not drunk. When the bombing started and the big guns on Gallaher's roof started, the noise was awful and we wanted Pop to come on to the nearest air raid shelter which was in Deacon St, just around the corner from our street, Crosscollyer St. He urged us to go on, saying we were young etc and if there was a bomb with his name on it he would take it at his own fireside. Of course we wouldn't leave him.

Bill Austin
Bangor, County Down

My mother sent me out to a shop that stayed open til eleven o'clock at night, she sent me out for a bag of biscuits. I was on my way back with the biscuits when I heard what appeared to be a machine gun going and a droning noise of an aeroplane. It wasn't flying very high, these boys found out very quickly there was no opposition and they came down and had a good look.

And then I heard soon after that particular droning noise of German twin diesel engine aircraft – could hear that quite distinctly. There was a policeman and he was with his tin hat on and he collared me and said 'get inside'. I spent the night with my mother, father and sister, we sat under the table not knowing what was happening.

Alfred Ambrose
Senior air-raid warden
Whitewell Road, north Belfast

Some time later the unsynchronised drone of enemy aircraft could be heard approaching from the direction of Knockagh Hill. It was a dark night and evidently the leaders were uncertain of their bearings, for they dropped flares. These slowly drifted in a north-easterly direction, eventually falling in Belfast Lough seemingly about Jordanstown or Whiteabbey. Still the engines droned overhead and Wardens gazing upwards felt defenceless and impotent. An uneasy feeling in the stomach hinted to us that we were scared, though no one admitted the fact openly at the time.

Further flares were dropped and this time they landed in and around the Post Area. While they were descending the whole area seemed brighter than noon in summer time.

I looked along the street and could recognise clearly two Wardens who were one hundred yards away. I felt as if I were standing in the street stark naked. As the flares touched the ground they were very promptly dealt with by Wardens who quickly had them extinguished. Ack ack fire opened up and I began to feel better, as I knew that 'Jerry' was not going to have it all his own way.

Ken Stanley
Antrim Road, north Belfast

On the Easter Tuesday we had all spent the day at the zoo, nice afternoon. I can remember going to bed about nine o'clock and being wakened by sound of sirens and grandfather shouting.

Tremendous noise and explosion and a couple of ceilings came down and we went out downstairs through the shop (shoemakers), where the whole front of the shop disappeared virtually. We ran to the air raid shelter in Hillman St. The smell and the noises. I was only out in the open for five minutes running from the house to the shelter but felt a whole multitude of emotions especially seeing St James Church in flames. Luckily we all got across and had shoes on because there was glass everywhere. St James Church was just a mass of flames and the school was also on fire.

When we got into the shelter there were about fifty people there already on seats all round the walls and people started to sing 'Run Rabbit Run'. There were maybe ten to fifteen children in the shelter and the adults were trying to put on a good face for the children and keep the spirits up.

Nellie Bell (née Gordon)
Crosscollyer Street, north Belfast

A landmine dropped in next street and our back door and kitchen window came in … Father shouted for his boots and pulled them on and we went to the air raid shelter pulling him along, nearly off his feet, and him urging us to leave him and save ourselves. He wasn't an old man but of course we sort of thought he was …

Anyhow the shelter was packed. This must have been about 12.30 or so when we arrived, and there we were all that night.

It was dreadful; we were all very quiet I think, I holding my father's hand and my new husband's. We stood. We could not sit down. It was pitch dark, I don't know who all were there, only I remember one wee man at the door of the shelter. Every time we heard the screeching of the falling bombs and the planes seemed to be just roof high, he always shouted 'don't worry, it's one of ours'. Some wit at the back shouted tell them we are here. I had no feeling in my feet and legs and I don't know what time it was but a landmine just missed the shelter and struck a row of houses in this street we were in. However when it was realized we were all 'safe' somebody started singing 'Nearer My God to Thee' and from then on it was hymns.

The planes had a 'free for all' – there was nothing to stop them, we found out later on. The odd anti-aircraft guns were so few they were wiped out in first half or so.

Moya Woodside
Elmwood Avenue, south Belfast

Where to begin? Dazed and mentally battered after five and a half hours of Blitz last night, one does not feel at one's most coherent. Sirens went about 10.30 p.m. as I was in the bath and the bombs started falling at 10.45. I went to bed and tried to sleep, but this proved impossible. After an hour or so one started listening and waiting for the bombs, wondering why the barrage wasn't louder and trying to analyse peculiar sounds. Nazi planes kept coming back, for all the world like some giant swarm of insects, whose drone was only ineffectually interrupted by bangs and crashes. For lengthy periods no noise could be heard but the planes kept flying about. One fretted 'why don't they fire at them' and 'where are our fighters?'

Emma Duffin
Voluntary Aid Detachment Commandant*
Stranmillis Military Hospital, south Belfast

I was wakened by the siren at 10.45 and almost instantaneously the anti-aircraft guns roared out. I hustled into my clothes and ran down the corridors to see that the girls were all awake and dressing and that all blackouts were up. I turned off the electricity at base every night, so that there was no possibility of anyone switching on an uncovered light.

The barrage grew more intense and the girls seemed to me incredibly slow about dressing, but dressing by torch light with rather trembling fingers is not easy. At last the sergeants and I had assured ourselves that all bedrooms were empty, and we followed the rest up to the kitchen and half-underground passages of Stranmillis House … It was an old-fashioned, well-built stone house, and the kitchen had steel beams across the ceiling which was rather reassuring.

The girls soon settled down. Some lay on shelves, others on tables, or the floor wrapped in their blankets. The day sisters had gone on duty but the VAD's [Voluntary Aid Detachment] instructions were to wait for orders … To my surprise, Matron remained with us. I had thought her place would have been in the main hospital. I could have well done without her … Although the blackouts were up, she said they fitted badly. She was, I must admit, right there for I could see the light of the flares the German planes were dropping through the cracks. On the other hand it was a beautiful moonlit night and as light as day outside.

---

* The Voluntary Aid Detachment largely consisted of middle-class female nursing staff employed in military hospitals.

William McCready
Librarian
Keadyville Avenue, Whiteabbey

It was in Keadyville Ave about midnight and I was sitting at the table trying to calculate how much in Income Tax I would pay in the next financial year. Suddenly I heard a long roaring whine and next moment a hell of a heavy thud. I went upstairs to the attic and standing on a box opened the skylight. Something in my stomach seemed to drop, for the whole length of the shipyard, for two to three miles, was ablaze with stark white light like the flash when taking a flash photograph.

Then guns, all over the city, began to roar. I knew it was our air raid. From the timber yards, about a mile from our house, flares were soon leaping in the sky. I was fascinated. A feeling of despair came over me – at last, I thought, it's our turn now, but I found myself engrossed by the spectacle. Closing the skylight I went downstairs to make sure the girls were all right – and then went out into the street, crossed York Road and went up Premier Drive which is a good deal higher than the main road. The whole sky in every direction was a mass of flame. The German planes taking part had now disappeared, but in half an hour I again heard the drone, very high in the sky, and many explosions followed.

Alfred Ambrose
Senior air-raid warden
Whitewell Road, north Belfast

The Senior Warden … came along Veryan Gardens on his way to the Post. A minute or two later he was outside the Post at 01.55 hrs with the Post Warden, who suddenly called

'Look out!' They had just time to fling themselves to the ground when a parachute mine fell in the centre of Veryan Gardens (opposite No. 44) with a vibrating crash which seemed to shatter the entire neighbourhood. This was followed almost immediately by another gigantic crash as a second parachute mine fell on open ground at the rear of 128 Whitewell Road. The Post Warden and Senior Warden had fallen just inside the entrance of the Post.

The roof of the Post was stripped, the ceiling crashed down, and the windows, door and telephone were hurled across the floor. It took a matter of seconds to turn off the gas at the meter, and scarcely had the Wardens collected their faculties after the severe blast, when they witnessed an appalling sight as some hundreds of people, verging on panic and many of them injured, came running down Whitewell Road towards the Post. This must be dealt with. The first task was to clear the roadway, which was done in a matter of minutes. Meanwhile, as the Post Warden dispatched his reports by messenger, the telephone being out of action, some twenty casualties were taken to Staghall House, which though severely damaged, had two or three rooms intact. Other casualties were dealt with at the Senior Warden's House by a CNR [Civil Nursing Reserve]* and Nurse assisted by a Lady Warden. Other casualties were placed in fields or in ditches, wherever cover could be found. A great number of casualties were treated at Graymount First Aid Post, and the Ambulance Officer and his Deputy worked like Trojans and dealt with scores of cases.

Meanwhile Wardens had been busy effecting immediate rescues of trapped or injured persons from houses only partly

---

* The Civil Nursing Reserve was established in January 1939 as part of the broader civil defence structure. It was staffed mainly by volunteers, most of whom worked as auxiliary and assistant nurses.

demolished. Passing from house to house they called out – 'Anybody there? Wardens here!' When answer was received the position was hastily explored, and with words of encouragement and the careful pulling aside of fallen timbers, quite a number of people were brought out, in some cases completely uninjured, from under the stairs of houses or other cavities.

At least ten small fires were quickly got out by Wardens. These fires were chiefly caused by blast entering the houses by the chimneys and scattering the coal fires in the grates throughout the rooms. This occurred in No. 45 Veryan Gardens, where the house had collapsed on eight persons of one family, but it was not known till long afterwards when the family had been extricated that they had all been killed instantaneously by blast. The head of this household, Mr Arthur Danby, was a Warden, and he was killed on his own doorstep where he had been posted by the Senior Warden. In this case the seat of the fire was beneath debris, and a human chain of buckets from the crater in the centre of the street, now filled with water, was inaugurated in an attempt to put out the fire.

PUBLIC NOTICE.

AFTER AN AIR RAID STAY UNDER COVER UNTIL YOU HEAR THE HANDBELLS.

THE "RAIDERS' PASSED" SIGNAL ON THE SIRENS (A CONTINUOUS BLAST) MEANS THAT ENEMY AIRCRAFT ARE BELIEVED TO HAVE LEFT THE AREA.

There will still exist a possible local danger from the presence of gas, unexploded bombs or dangerous buildings after a bombing attack, and members of the Public should remain under cover until they hear the "All Clear" signal which will be given in all cases by Wardens ringing their handbells.

The Wardens will, on hearing the "Raiders' Passed" signal, patrol their Sectors and ascertain that it is safe before sounding the handbells and the Public should not take the continuous blast on the sirens as indicating that all danger is passed.

WAIT UNTIL YOU HEAR THE HANDBELLS BEFORE LEAVING COVER

James Kelly
Northern Political Editor, Irish Independent
Glen Road, west Belfast

I have a vivid memory of walking home in the blackout from the trolley-bus stop at the end of the Glen Road when the sirens went at 11.40 p.m. It was a mild night with only a small amount of white cloud and a light breeze. I had just reached the open fields at the city boundary when I heard the unfamiliar heavy 'bub-bub-bub' sound of aircraft approaching from the south east. As the noise got closer my instinct that the menacing sound spelt danger was confirmed when suddenly a couple of anti-aircraft guns crashed into life. Quickening my pace I reached home to find the family late-night supper had been abandoned as the realisation dawned that we were, at last, about to experience an attack from the air with God knows what consequences.

We could hear more and more planes droning overhead and we waited with bated breath, wondering when some unknown airman would press the button releasing his deadly load of high explosives on the hapless victims below. Worst of all was the nerve-shattering sound of the anti-aircraft guns which seemed closer than we had realised. They sounded like iron fists pounding on the front door which rattled on its hinges and we looked anxiously at the windows as they too shook with each detonation. Soon there were other sounds from the city five miles away from our suburb.

Every minute or two came the dull boom and echo of bombs landing on their targets, the din increasing in intensity as the attack was pressed home by new waves of bombers. Down there in the city, people were being killed, homes destroyed and buildings levelled to the ground. We prayed for them and for ourselves for who knew when one of the aircraft homing in on the city might release its load out in the suburb and fly back to base?

William McCready
Librarian
Keadyville Avenue, Whiteabbey

Returning to the house and going up again to the attic I pushed the skylight right over until it was resting on the slates, and from this vantage point I could see the shell fire from all over the city accompanied by the 'flaming onions'. Very high in the sky I could see the balloons: they looked tiny and lovely. Across the glare in the sky I saw a solitary seagull and felt rather sorry for it and all the other birds. From time to time the house shook and the windows and doors rattled. It went on like this til 3.00 a.m. and then came an uneasy quietness. The only sounds now came from the terrific fires and from distant voices and from the fire engines. We decided we would go to bed and after another look around the house, I undressed and lay down in bed, but there came another terrific explosion.

Doreen Bates
Sydenham, east Belfast

From 11.00 to 04.00, with scarcely a break of ten minutes, German planes kept coming over dropping heavy stuff and must have been heavy having regard to the degree of vibration and the distance which was sufficient to prevent the windows here in the neighbourhood from being broken. The AA [anti-aircraft] kept up a continuous barrage but it could not even keep them high. You could hear them dive before releasing their bombs. Our fighters were up and at times there was incessant machine gunning. It was the worst night I have had here or at Purley. The Bennetts came down to my room and I made tea. At 01.20 I went to bed, thinking I was as safe there as anywhere, and though it was impossible to sleep I should be resting physically.

Several times the bed swayed like a cot being rocked; doors and windows rattled; shrapnel patted on the shed roof outside; I could see against the blackout the glare of the fires. The most nerve-wracking thing to me was when the Germans glided in silently and the only sound was the crump of bombs. I went over poems in my head, they seemed even lovelier and more permanent in that inferno. Having exhausted those I could remember I went onto hymns and psalms, but I could remember fewer of those.

Reverend Eric Gallagher
Woodvale Methodist Church
Cambrai Street, west Belfast

We had an underground heating chamber, which we turned into an air raid shelter. I remember one woman crying her eyes out, worrying about her friend Tilly. I said I would go and look for Tilly, and when I found her said her friend wanted to see her. She was very nervous about leaving, but I eventually persuaded her to go to the shelter.

I had her by the arm, helping her along in her nervousness, but as we crossed the street there was a rattle on roofs opposite – shrapnel from anti-aircraft guns. Tilly stopped dead. She wouldn't move another inch forward and made to run straight back home. When I asked her why, she said she had to go back – she'd left her budgie in the kitchen.

Iris Rocks
Broom Street, west Belfast

Everybody was out and we walked up the Ballygomartin Rd and up the Glencairn Rd, which was a country road. It was all trees and every family got under a tree and we all stayed together and sat on the ground and watched the blazing from the streets near us.

The sky was red with flames, awful awful, desperate children holding tight to their parents and they were literally shaking. And when the All Clear sounded the Ballygomartin Rd was crowded with people all saying to themselves things like 'we'll never get over this'.

Moya Woodside
Elmwood Avenue, south Belfast

At 3 a.m. I could stand it no longer and feeling desperately frightened and somewhat hysterical, put on a dressing gown and went down to join my husband in his vigil below the stairs. I grabbed the whiskey decanter, and with shaking hands drank off about a quarter tumbler neat to try and pull myself together. (Usually I dislike whiskey and I never touch it.) We then sat down in the pantry under the stairs, and just waited. After a while I recovered my self-control, and began to reflect mournfully that this – this was civilisation in 1941. Sitting, shivering, bored and frightened in a cubby hole at 3.30 a.m.

John Morrow
Ivanhoe Street, south Belfast

With every blast the slatted seat beneath moved (as it was supposed to; the shelters had no foundations) and, in between, blasts of air sang like cut wire and we could hear the beat of aero engines.

Mr Wilson, who suffered from Parkinson's disease, stood shaking in the doorway and after every blast he shouted 'that's one of ours now!' Then, with the raids still on, soldiers turned us out of the shelter because of an unexploded bomb near the main tank in the gasworks.

Clutching father's hand, hurrying up the Ormeau Rd to my aunt's in Hatfield St, I looked back and saw shapes passing low in the red sky over the city. Mr Wilson ran past, pointing, screaming 'It's one of ours.' Only long after did we learn that there had been none, of anything, of ours.

John Kelly
Dublin Fire Brigade

It was very cold and I nearly froze riding that open engine to Belfast. I had to sit on my hands to keep them from getting numb. There were no landmarks on the way up; we reached our destination by following the telephone lines. The fires in Belfast were the worst I've ever seen in my life. The whole area was in ruins and there were human bodies and dead animals lying all over the place. On the way home we stopped in Newry for a drink and when the local people learnt who we were, they gave us a great welcome. They all wanted souvenirs and by the time we got out of the place, none of us had a button left on our tunics.

3rd Officer Laurence Carrol
Dublin Fire Brigade

I was 'phone operator in Dorset Street station and took the call from HQ asking for volunteers to go to Belfast. I couldn't believe it and checked back to get it confirmed. We were directed to a fire in a margarine factory, but I hadn't a clue where it was … and I've never found out. The whole place was chaos; mind you they did the best they could. In Belfast we were treated very decently and they came round with canteen cars to feed us. But what I'll never forget was seeing the dead bodies being loaded into lorries.

Lady Lilian Spender
Stormont, east Belfast

It lasted five hours and we were devoutly thankful to have the strong room so comparatively hospitable. Some sat or lay on the shelves, and some on stools on the floor, on every variety of wrap and coat and rug and slumbercap. I did the longest piece of non-stop knitting I have ever achieved, and Daffodil immersed herself in *Anna Karenina*. I needn't describe it, even if I were allowed to, as you all know far more about such things than we do!!

We went to bed finally about 04.00 and about 05.00 a despatch rider arrived to let Wolf know that the 'state of emergency' had been declared and the Ministry of Public Security taken control, as previously arranged.

Hugh Dixon
Clifton Park Avenue, north Belfast

Dear Bill,

I hope this reaches you, and that it finds you and Edie and kiddies all well and happy … We are all ok. The two kiddies are evacuated to the country, Louie is a telephonist in the army, and Nan is at home with Lucy and I. I'm sorry it's not permissible to send you a photo of Louie in her uniform. She looks real smart …

To those who haven't experienced one, it's difficult to

appreciate what a 'Blitz' is like … Imagine you're just finished supper and are having a smoke before retiring. Suddenly, the stillness of the night is rudely disturbed by an eerie wailing sound – the sirens. Your pulse quickens, your heart thumps; you rush upstairs and fill the bath and a couple of water buckets, and see that all the windows are properly blacked-out whilst your wife and daughter see to the sand-bags, the gas masks and the long handle rakes for dealing with incendiaries.

The initial shock has passed, you light a cigarette and advise the wife and daughter to run to the public shelters, saying that you are going to stay to look after the house; but they won't go without you, so into the little cloak-room under the stairs you go. All precautions taken, you walk out to the garden gate. Men and women are hurrying along the street to the shelters, ARP [Air Raid Precautions] workers are hurrying to their posts, motors and other vehicles are flying up and down the roads. You glance up at the sky and curse the bright moon, at the same time wondering whether the smoke screen thrown up by the oil fires the military are lighting will blot it out.

All the while you stand watching and listening; then you hear the planes away in the distance. Our own or Germans? You scan the skies but see nothing; then you hear what sounds like machine gun fire. Our night fighters are at them. You watch and listen. The planes are coming nearer and nearer. You hurry into the cloak-room. You sit crouched under the stairs, waiting and listening. They're coming nearer and nearer. Then the anti-aircraft guns open out. What a din. It's like hell let loose. For the moment you feel delighted. That'll blast the beggars from the sky. But, no. You can still hear the planes coming nearer and nearer. Despite the terrific barrage from our guns, you can still hear the planes. They seem to be right overhead. They seem to be circling round and round. Suddenly the sound of their engines ceases. They're diving down. You hold your breath for five, six seconds; then swish – a thin screechy whistling sound. The high explosives are coming.

You close your eyes and crouch. Bang. Bang. Bang. Bang. Crash. Some of your windows upstairs are shattered by the blast, some of the plaster drops from the ceiling. But you breathe a sigh of relief. You're safe. Though some of the bombs must have dropped pretty close. Bang. Bang. Bang. Bang. Down they come again. Suddenly, there's a more terrifying bang. The very earth quakes. More windows are shattered, a door blown off its hinges, the whole house rocks. My God! A landmine. Fifteen minutes of this, and then all noise ceases. That crowd has been beaten off. You venture out to the garden gate and glance down the street. Ambulances and Fire Brigades are flying down the road. Away to the north and the south the sky is a dull red. Big fires somewhere. From a nearby shelter you hear the crowd singing 'There'll always be an England'. You venture up the avenue a little and look up another street. In the distance you can see steel-helmeted men and nurses rushing about. As your eyes grow accustomed to the darkness you see that what was formerly a street of semi-detached houses is now a mere mass of debris.

A policeman hurries down the street. Much damage done? you ask him. Land mine, direct hit, about 30 houses demolished, he replies. Many killed? you ask. 'Fraid so, he answers, hurrying on. You stand watching, then you hear the planes gain. You search the skies, but see nothing. They come nearer and nearer. A flare is dropped. It lights about 1,000 feet up in the air. It lights up the whole sky. What a spectacle. You see out balloon barrage quite clearly. They look funny. Just like silvery elephants without legs strung up in the air. But you cannot see any planes. You hurry back to the house. You can hear them coming nearer and nearer. The anti-aircraft guns open out again. But still the planes come on. They seem to be circling right over your head. A series of dull thuds! Incendiaries. You rush into the kitchen, into the sitting-room, upstairs and into each of the bed-rooms to see if any of them have dropped into the house. From the window you see an amazing spectacle. One has dropped into your garden, several have dropped into the road, two have dropped into a house down the street. All blazing fiercely. You rush downstairs, grab the sandbag, and rush out to the garden. As you approached the incendiary the heat scorches your face. You duck your head, hold the sand bag in front of your face for protection, and edge closer and closer. Then you dump the sandbag right on top of the bomb. You glance down the street. Two houses are blazing away. Fire fighters are dealing with dozens of other incendiaries that have dropped in the road. Swish! The thin screechy whistle.

You rush towards the house. As you're running up the hall – Bang! Bang! Bang! You're violently hurled against the wall and fall to the floor. For the moment you're stunned, but you quickly recover as you realise that it was merely the blast from a bomb that has dropped a hundred yards away. Back crouching under the stairs again. And still they come. You stick it for five minutes, then curiosity overcomes your discretion. You venture out to the back garden to see what's going on. Searchlights are moving across the sky. You watch. Suddenly you hold your breath. They've caught a plane in the beam. You watch fascinated. The plane soars up but the beam follows. It dives down, but the beam holds it. Why the hell doesn't the guns open out on it! They do. It's like hell with the lid off. Shells bursting all round the plane. It soars, it dives, it swerves in a frantic effort to get away from the

Section of a bomb crater in Ravenscroft Avenue, Newtownards Road, in the east of the city.

beam of the searchlight. Still the shells burst all round it. Damn it. It has got away. But no. The beam picks it up again. It seems to be losing height. Smoke seems to be coming from it. Another terrific barrage of shells all round it. It's on fire. It's zig-zagging. It's out of control. It's all ablaze. It's coming straight down. Hope it doesn't drop in the city. Suddenly all become silent. That squadron have been chased. You go inside, and make a cup of tea. You have just taken it into the cloak-room, when you again hear the planes coming.

And so it goes on, hour after hour, until shortly before dawn. Then what a relief. You hear the All Clear. You crawl out and stretch your cramped limbs a moment, then you all go out to the front gate … Tired, sleepy men, women and children are hurrying from the shelters to their homes. ARP workers are also rushing about.

Alfred Ambrose
Senior air-raid warden
Whitewell Road, north Belfast

Now we had time to make a reconnaissance of the area. Numerous houses were demolished and hundreds damaged. It was still dark but the task on hand was obviously greater than we could handle unaided. A Dispatch Rider left with a message to 'B' Group Posts asking for the help of all available Wardens. School-rooms were opened as Rest Centres, where ladies carried out invaluable work in supplying tea for the homeless and keeping hundreds of people off the streets. The 'B' Group Wardens received our SOS message at 04.54 hours, and we shall be ever grateful to them for their splendid response. When these reinforcements arrived, daylight was breaking, and the scene was one of orderly activity.

In Veryan Gardens an ambulance was being loaded on one side of the crater. On the other side a lorry was drawn up being loaded with dead, which were being taken to Erskine's Felt Works, where a temporary mortuary had been established. The Senior Warden had control of the position and was in close touch with all that was taking place.

An electric cable lay on the surface from the crater and across the mound of slippery wet clay surrounding it. Assuming that it might be a live cable a Warden was posted to warn all persons approaching it to beware of the live cable. Many stretcher-bearers had to cross the cable and these were warned each time they approached the danger. One stretcher-bearer slipped on the clay as he was about to step over the cable – and it was live! A flash shot up his leg, but fortunately he was not injured. Later, the current was cut off.

James Kelly
Northern Political Editor, Irish Independent
Glen Road, west Belfast

The Glen Road is on high ground flanking the western hills and below us lay the city now a sea of flames across the horizon. Ghostly flares cast a blinding white light as they floated like sinister candelabra tearing the dark veil of night apart, revealing the spires, chimneys and high buildings waiting pathetically for their fate. Searchlights and the 'flaming onions' from the shipyard dockside aircraft carrier, HMS Furious, fortuitously in Belfast for repairs, ripped through the sky at the unseen targets but it seemed that the city was helpless as every so often there was another dull boom and we could see a cauldron of flame and smoke, as from a volcano, shoot upwards.

The defences seemed to peter out after an hour. The

bombers had the city at their mercy until about 3.00 a.m. when people crowded out onto the road and gazed at the awesome sight of a city enveloped in a sea of flames. There was a stricken silence among the onlookers until one hoarse voice exclaimed 'My God. That's Belfast finished.' After a few hours' sleep I prepared to drive into the city to try to pick up the pieces for a major news story for the Dublin *Evening Herald.* For a newspaper man the show must go on however appalled and stunned you might feel by happenings around you. I noticed wads of burnt paper lying in other back garden and on examining them I was surprised to find that they were invoices from a commercial concern at Prince's Dock, five miles away. Presumably they had been blown into the sky by a bomb-hit and wafted by a breeze to the Glen Road slopes.

Emma Duffin
Voluntary Aid Detachment Commandant
Stranmillis Military Hospital, south Belfast

I speculated that if any of the girls got hysterical or needy, sitting in the dark would not be good for their morale, yet if one even put on a small pocket torch to look at a watch, she [the Matron] called out to them to extinguish it. Meanwhile the noise of the barrage and the thuds of falling bombs continued. We realised this was a real 'Blitz' but not till the next day did we know how very severe it had been. Some of the girls went to sleep and snored loudly, others talked almost incessantly …

Owing to the dark, I could not see that everyone was there but knew nobody had been left in the quarters. There were slight pauses, but not of long duration. I sat in a kitchen chair … with my steel helmet on and my gas mask on my shoulders. I would much rather have been on duty. The night seemed interminable. It was not till nearly 6 a.m. that we heard the welcome sound of the All Clear.

When we emerged we saw the sky red with the reflection from fires, and realised there must be a good deal of damage.

Holy Family Parish Chronicle
Newington Avenue, north Belfast

The air raid sirens sounded and the city experienced one of the heavy 'blitzes'. This parish of Holy Family suffered very heavily. The raid lasted almost six hours. Thanks to the good work done by Fr Walls a large number of incendiary bombs, which fell about the church grounds, were extinguished. Towards the end of the raid a high explosive bomb fell on Nos 30 and 32 Atlantic Avenue, demolishing the backs of both houses and severely damaging the Gate Lodge of Holy Family Parish, and also the Hall and the entrance gates.

A remarkable escape of death was seen in the fact that the local caretaker James McGrath left the Lodge with his wife and children when the raid was at its height and ran to the shelter in Atlantic Avenue. This shelter was demolished as a result of blast from a HE* bomb which fell about thirty ft away and fourteen people were killed.

McGrath, his wife and family escaped with slight injuries. As far as we know only one Catholic woman was killed, a lady called Murray, a visitor from Antrim town who had been in Belfast to see friends.

---

* High Explosive bomb, as opposed to an incendiary bomb. There were HE bombs of various sizes, though almost all were fitted with a thin casing and simple impact fuse in order to create the greatest possible explosion when they fell.

Ken Stanley
Antrim Road, north Belfast

Anyway about three or four in the morning the All Clear came, and we came round and walked onto Antrim Rd – you could hear the cracking of timber from St James' [Church].

Between Hillman St and Duncairn Gds there were three very large houses and they simply disappeared, they had taken the full force of the landmines. And I remember seeing the rubble there and the flames.

But my abiding memory was looking up and seeing the parachute of the landmine hanging from the tram wires and we weren't aware til later on that in those three houses people had been killed … We came back to what was left of our house and we spent a couple of days there. Grandfather had relations in Lisburn and we spent a couple of weeks there.

That day we were told that the blast from the landmine had moved the roof off the shelter so it was only hanging by about 2 cms from collapsing on people below.

Sam Hanna Bell
Crescent Gardens, south Belfast

After the All Clear we reported at our sector headquarters, and there we were told that a bomb, a parachute bomb, had gone off down near the river damaging a row of houses on the Antrim side rather badly, and would half a dozen of us volunteer to go over and see if we could be of any use.

The damage wasn't as bad as we had expected. A lot of slates off and doors and windows blown in but no brickwork down. There wasn't a soul to be seen, now maybe they'd been got out before the thing went off or maybe it was one of those streets that took to the hills every night. Another warden and I went into the first house; the blast had lifted the street door and wedged it half way down the hall. With a certain amount of pushing and grunting we got it unwedged and propped against the wall, and then we heard a voice. We both made a dive for the little door under the stairs and there huddled away in the darkest corner was an old woman nursing something on her knee. It might have been a flask or a cat or a hot water bottle. 'Have you chased them away, sons?' she said. We got her out, dusted her down and told her they'd gone. When we got the light going in the scullery we saw what the old soul had been clutching through that frightful night – it was a wee Union Jack on a stick.

BELFAST NEWS LETTER

A Week of
Horrors

The official account of the Belfast Blitz (published in the British Ministry of Information for the Minister of Home Security) describes how on the morning after the seven-hour heavy bombardment of Belfast on the night of 15 April, parts of the city 'were a gruesome sight'. Ruin-fringed roads were blocked by heaps of smouldering debris and acrid-smelling craters. Emergency feeding centres and rest centres providing meals and washing facilities sprang up all over the city to cater for the seventy thousand people who needed assistance.

Government and municipal officials struggled to give accurate information on the number of dead and wounded, as both the recovery of human remains and the logging of information were shambolic. The limited mortuary services were so overstretched that the Falls Road Swimming Baths had to be drained and used as a makeshift mortuary. It was here and at St George's Market that the dead were laid out for identification by family and relatives.

Even as the public funerals of the unclaimed bodies were taking place in the Milltown and City cemeteries on Monday 21 April, more human remains were being found and new estimates of the number of dead released. Given the chaos of the time and the sclerotic official response it's impossible to reach an accurate number of those killed on the Easter Tuesday raid but most estimates agree it was between eight and nine hundred.

Looking after the living and reassuring them it was safe to stay in the city was now a real challenge for public officials. One cause for concern was what would happen in further raids if dangerous animals escaped from Bellevue Zoo. In order to 'reassure the public and calm fears of local residents' it was decided that twenty-three animals, among them lions, bears, wolves, and a tiger, should be destroyed. Two marksmen, one from the Royal Ulster Constabulary, the other from the Home Guard, carried out the shootings while Dick Foster, head keeper, watched with 'tears streaming down his face, as the executioners proceeded from cage to cage'.

But there were deeper problems. In January 1941 Air Raid Precautions had made arrangements, in the event of a blitz on Belfast, for homeless people to be accommodated in church and school halls across the city. Blankets and emergency stocks of food had been supplied to the sites and caretakers were informed that should a raid occur the halls were to be made ready. But the people of Belfast thought otherwise.

Many of the observers noted the mass exodus from Belfast that occurred after the Easter Tuesday raid, as those fortunate enough to have relatives in country areas willing to accommodate them, headed to rural safety. This exodus contained both the bombed out – those whose houses had been destroyed – and the scared out – those whose houses were habitable but who lived in fear.

A huge proportion of Belfast residents refused to sleep in their own homes at night, preferring instead to trek into the hills all around Belfast to sleep in open fields or even in ditches. The 'ditchers', as they soon became known, lived in fear and headed to any place they assumed would give them safety. Their evening exodus gave the government a new problem – abysmally low morale among the civilian population who feared another devastating raid.

Nellie Bell (née Gordon)
Married to Bob Bell on Easter Monday, 1941
Crosscollyer Street, north Belfast

The death and destruction that night was horrific … I'll never forget when the All Clear went and we came out the whole sky was pink. I don't think it was just dawn, there were fires everywhere and ambulances and fire engines roaring all over the place …

We could hardly walk we were so stiff and cold and of course shocked. We were afraid to look round the corner as we came to our house, we couldn't imagine it would still be there, but there it was. The whole gable end was cracked and the windows all broken and inside was awful. The few [wedding] presents we had got were buried under the glass and dirt from the bay window which was caved in …

Bob was very anxious about his mother … who lived top of Springfield Rd with Madge in her shop. Father and Bob and me set off to walk there, there was no transport of course. The whole way along it was terrible. At top of Duncairn Gdns there had been a direct hit on a shelter and all were killed.

People coming from a dance at Floral Hall had got off the tram when things got so bad and went there for safety. I knew three girls who were killed. I didn't know that then, but as we passed the dead and injured were being brought out.

The Phoenix bar on Antrim Rd was standing, no doors or windows on it. We went in and had a drink and then went on our way right across to Springfield. They were all safe, they had spent the night up the road, there were no houses built at that time. It was open country and considered safe, people went up there every night after that for months. Any place not built on was where people went.

I had not shed a tear the whole time but when we got to Springfield after all the things I'd seen on the way and the whole trauma of it all, I was physically sick in the bathroom and cried and cried. Mrs Bell really scolded me and said I should be glad we were all alive and I suppose she was right but I felt she was very unkind. I know she was right but it took a long time to forgive her for barging me as she did. I was only married after all. All my dreams and hopes and we didn't know what more was going to happen.

Doreen Bates
Tax Inspector
Sydenham, east Belfast

This morning it was good to be alive and I enjoyed every crumb of breakfast, I listened to the 08.00 news to hear what the family would learn and decided to write, reassuring them at once. It was amazing after that noise to find not a tile off or window broken till I had gone some distance to the office towards Belfast.

Alfred Ambrose
Senior air-raid warden
Whitewell Road, north Belfast

With daybreak crowds of spectators began to collect and, with the assistance of the police, cordons of ropes were placed across the approaches to the damaged area, and only persons who could satisfy the guards that they had vital business inside the area were allowed within the roped-off area. This ban was, however, tempered with kindness and relatives of missing persons and those whose homes had been damaged were given every consideration.

On account of the large number of identity cards which had already been found in the neighbourhood, it was considered essential that these alone should not be accepted as proof of identity, but that persons seeking to enter houses or remove personal effects should first be identified by a local Warden or policeman. This system worked quite satisfactorily.

Some remarkable escapes were experienced. In Veryan Gardens two ladies and a little boy were rescued after their home had collapsed on them. This work was carried out in darkness with the splendid assistance of military. The Senior Warden crawled through and under debris from the back of the house and directed the work. One of the ladies was pinned by a floor joist which had to be sawn through before she could be extricated.

Hugh Dixon
Clifton Park Avenue, north Belfast

You come to a street cordoned off. You edge in amongst the crowd. Direct hit on a shelter, someone remarks. Many in it? you ask. About fifty, is the reply. You stand watching the salvage workers frenziedly working amongst the debris. One of them shouts. Others rush over to him. They work feverishly to lever up some heavy slab of concrete. You feel a sickly sensation in the stomach. You know they're trying to get at some bodies. They're gently dragging at something. It's a woman. She seems bent in two, probably spine smashed. As they turn her over, a nurse rushes forward. There's a child in the woman's arms. It's alive. Evidently the mother has sheltered the infant with her own body. With a choking sensation in your throat, you turn away. You pass the hospital. A procession of stretcher cases going in, men and women coming out with heads bandaged or arms in a sling. You think of the tireless devotion to duty of the doctors and nurses. You think of the courage of the ordinary men and women. There's a lot of good in human nature after all. Other pale-faced men and sobbing women are coming out of the hospital. You know they've learned the worst about their dear ones. On down to work, but near the works the road is cordoned off and the military in charge. No work today, you learn. Dozens of time bombs and unexploded mines all around the place. You meet work-mates, and exchange experiences. You learn about poor Jim. Direct hit on house. He and wife and family of six all killed. Lucky Bob. He had a miraculous escape. House demolished, but he escaped with a few scratches. You turn homewards. Tension now relaxed, the reaction sets in. You're sleepy, leg-weary, depressed and with a peculiar feeling in your stomach. You hope the night-workers club will be open. You need a drink. It's crowded. You push your way up to the bar and order a double whiskey. You gulp it down. It might as well be lemonade for all the effect it has on you. You have another and another. You feel a little brighter and home you go. And so to bed for a good sleep in case the beggars come back again that night.

Major Seán O'Sullivan
Air Raid Precautions observer from Dublin

In the Antrim Road [north Belfast] and vicinity the attack was of a particularly concentrated character and in many instances bombs from successive waves of bombers fell within fifteen to twenty yards of one another. In this general area, scores of houses were completely wrecked, either by explosion, fire or blast, while hundreds were damaged so badly as to be uninhabitable.

In suburban areas, many were allowed to burn themselves

out and during the day wooden beams were still burning. During the night of 16th/17th, many of these smouldering fires broke out afresh and fire appliances could be heard passing throughout the night ... It is estimated that the ultimate number of dead may be in the neighbourhood of five hundred, and final figures may even approach two thousand ...

The rescue service felt the want of heavy jacks; in one case the leg and arm of a child had to be amputated before it could be extricated ... [But] the greatest want appeared to be the lack of hospital facilities.

At 2 p.m., on the afternoon of the 16th (nine hours after the termination of the raid), it was reported that the street leading to the Mater Hospital was filled with ambulances waiting to set down their casualties ... Professor Flynn [father of actor, Errol Flynn], head of the casualty service for the city, informed me that the greater number of casualties was due to shock, blast and secondary missiles, such as glass, stones, pieces of piping, etc.

There were many terrible mutilations among both living and dead – heads crushed, ghastly abdominal and face wounds, penetration by beams, mangled and crushed limbs, etc. ... In the heavily 'blitzed' areas people ran panic-stricken into the streets and made for the open country.

As many were caught in the open by blast and secondary missiles, the enormous number of casualties can be readily accounted for. It is perhaps true that many saved their lives running but I am afraid a much greater number lost them or became casualties.

During the day, loosened slates and pieces of piping were falling in the streets and as pedestrians were numerous many casualties must have occurred.

Emma Duffin
Voluntary Aid Detachment Commandant
Stranmillis Military Hospital, south Belfast

Everyone went on duty as usual next day. We learnt that several incendiary bombs had fallen in the hospital grounds and in the Stranmillis Road. The milkman brought news of objectives which had been hit. Girls whose people were in vulnerable areas were anxious, and tore off in their off duty time to learn the extent of the damage. Two of them and two of the kitchen maids had had their homes demolished, but their people were safe.

One girl came back, with a green face and eyes like saucers, her home was gone, her people at a rest centre, but she had seen the dead body of a child carried from the ruins of a house and it had shaken her. Bit by bit news of the extensive damage reached us. Harland and Wolff, Victoria Barracks, Ewart's Mill, Dixons Timber Yard. Some reports were exaggerated, but it was obvious a good deal of damage had been done …

We got few casualties, most of them going to the civilian hospitals which were very full. I went to the Donegall Rd Military Hospital to see how my VADs there had stood it. I stopped first at the billets and saw the lady cook. She was a very young girl and had been left alone in the house with some young maids, as the sisters had all gone on duty. She seemed to have stood it well, but said she would have liked a steel helmet – and one of the maids had been badly scared. There was no shelter and they had just stayed in the hall. Some of the VAD had been left in the other part of the quarters on the opposite side of the road and the cook reported one had been badly scared, so I proceeded to the hospital to enquire. The hospital was really a wing of the Infirmary, and one passed through the Workhouse Gates to reach it. At the gate was a pony. I learnt later it had brought the dead bodies to the Infirmary mortuary and some of the VADs had been upset by seeing them brought in …

I talked to several of the other girls, who looked tired but calm, but one poor child, who also came from Éire, looked dazed and shaken. 'I don't really know what I'm doing,' she said, 'and the Sister of the wards has been recalled to another hospital where there are casualties. Oh am I glad to see you.' 'You'll have to keep calm, if sister's gone they'll depend on you,' I said, but I felt a bit worried about her. She had been ill recently and [her] very agitated and funny mother had arrived from Queen's County. She referred to her always as 'Bubbles' and spoke of how marvellous 'Bubbles' had been in air raids at Bristol and what a wonderful nurse she was.

Actually she was unsuited to be a nurse, as she was untidy and messy, and never got good reports, though she was a nice child to speak to and meant well. I began to wonder whether poor 'Bubbles' had stood up to the air-raids in Bristol as well as her fond mother imagined.

She was going to our house to tea the next day, so I slipped round after tea to see how she was. She still looked dazed, and her clothes were put on anyway, her shoes were filthy and even her hands looked dirty. She told me she had felt cold and shivery ever since the Blitz so, as she had a half day, I advised her to go to bed with a hot drink and hot water bag.

Alfred Ambrose
Senior air-raid warden
Whitewell Road, north Belfast

Throughout the day of Easter Wednesday the rescue work proceeded without interruption. A Rescue Squad carried out excellent work in turning over the crashed houses, brick by brick, and timber by timber, into the spaces which had

A group of soldiers take a much-needed break amid the rubble.

formerly been the gardens. After watching the procedure adopted by the Rescue Squad, teams of Wardens were employed in carrying out the same procedure at other houses. Only about three men could be employed at each house, as it was found that when more were at work the extra men got in the way of the others. This work proceeded very rapidly and it was surprising how quickly the entire fabric of one of these 'subsidy' houses could be turned over.

As the search among the debris continued many items of small personal effects, including jewellery, money, Savings Banks books, insurance policies, wills, letters and so on, were unearthed and were handed to the Wardens' officers, who used a pillow-case to hold the small effects brought out of each separate house. When they had accumulated a number of these bags, each with the name and address of the householder inside, they were taken by a responsible officer to the Police Barracks, where they were kept in safe-keeping, until a later day when the contents were examined and listed in the presence of representatives of the Police and of the Wardens' Service.

Although the Civil Defence personnel had been out all night and had been working at pressure speed from the early hours of the morning, I heard no word of complaint regarding tiredness or hunger. When a Civil Defence Mobile Canteen arrived, the Civil Defence personnel, although their tongues were cleaving to the roofs of their mouths with dust from the debris, promptly decided to give first priority to the military who had given such fine voluntary help.

When the soldiers had received tea and sandwiches, it was found that the Canteen used the last water available. The Canteen ladies said 'Get us water and we will give you tea.' But the water mains were gone and the supply was by then cut off. From the corner of a severely damaged house hung its storage cistern some fifteen feet above ground level, and the overflow pipe was spilling water in a long trickle which swayed to and fro in the breeze. By skilful manoeuvring of a bucket beneath this trickle sufficient water was eventually collected to fulfil requirements. I have never enjoyed refreshment so much as I did that mug of strong sweet tea and those thick meat sandwiches. I suppose I had never before needed a meal so much.

Belfast News Letter
18 April 1941

Belfast is recovering from the effects of the air raid on Tuesday night. Considerable progress was made yesterday with the clearing of debris from the bombed areas. Many more bodies were recovered and homeless people were found alternative accommodation in more fortunate districts. The first stunning blow of the attack having passed, people turned to the task of adapting themselves to the altered conditions and generally met the change with renewed confidence.

Mobile Canteens

Mobile canteens toured the bombed areas throughout the day and distributed free meals to those whose homes had suffered in the raid. In this way the people benefited by their own past generosity, for most of the canteens had been purchased by public subscriptions to bring refreshments to troops stationed in the Province.

Thousands of meals were provided. Each canteen carries about 200 cups and tea sufficient for almost a thousand people. Large quantities of bread in proportion was also distributed.

The canteen handed over to the Salvation Army by his Grace the Governor of Northern Ireland and another provided by the residents of Londonderry were among those which contributed to this great relief work. The people were unstinted [sic] in their appreciation of this help, and the canteen staffs received many touching words of gratitude. One canteen worker told a *News Letter* reporter that the chivalry of the people was wonderful; way was always made for women with children in their arms and for the aged and infirm. Many offers of help were also received from women in the damaged areas.

Hot Meals

Hot meals were served at thirty-three official rest centres, and at many others established in schools, church halls, and other large buildings where teachers, members of the Women's Auxiliary Service, and scores of volunteers catered for the comfort of victims of the Nazi viciousness.

The numbers to be dealt with exceeded expectations upon which the original arrangements were made, but facilities were speedily extended, many new centres were opened, and the staffs worked ungrudgingly for exhausting periods, so that none should be turned away or left uncared for.

The great majority of those needing assistance were women with large families of young children. Clothing was given to many, and, in many cases, playthings were found for the children. In a surprisingly short time the homeless settled down in their temporary quarters.

A reporter writes: 'I had a talk last night with the lady helper who toured the bombed areas of Belfast in the YMCA mobile canteen presented by the residents of Londonderry. The people of Derry must be gratified that their generosity has brought succour to thousands of their fellow Ulstermen and Ulster families. She told me that every one of the two hundred cups carried in the canteen had been in use from eleven o'clock in the morning until late in the evening. The people themselves were as helpful as could be, she said. One of the canteen's stopping places was opposite a fish-and-chip shop which had been damaged. The owner was there and noticed the gratitude of the crowd as tea and bread were distributed. He went into the shop and took out his stock of fish and chips and handed it over to the canteen where the fish and chips were heated and distributed to those waiting. A cheer went up from the crowd.'

Norman Kennedy
Holywood Arches, east Belfast

My father was in the ARP [Air Raid Precautions] at the bottom of Holywood Arches and my sister was a telephonist there was as well. On Easter Tuesday, the first of the big raids, we were under the stairs, the noise was appalling you could feel the houses vibrating.

I went down the Albertbridge Road the morning after and you were tripping over fire hoses: you weren't allowed down Thorndyke St for example, they had very, very heavy casualties. I remember going down as far as Templemore Avenue and seeing boilers and beds hanging out of back wall of the hospital there. It was very, very exciting. Boys, my friends, scavenged round picking up shrapnel up and down the Avenue. That changed the whole aspect of East Belfast.

Moya Woodside
Elmwood Avenue, south Belfast

Went downtown on my bike shopping. Atmosphere completely different from the morning after our previous 'sample' raid last week. People are quiet and look harassed and weary. 'Isn't it awful' is the most frequent comment. There seems less tendency to dilate our personal experiences. Everyone is asking; 'why don't we have a proper barrage. They did just as they liked.' …

Centre of town comparatively undamaged, number of plate glass windows gone, several areas roped off for time bombs. People are shopping with anxious faces, but there is little to buy, for as well as Blitz dislocation it's the day after the holiday. Blackened faces, bandaged heads, parties of mothers and children with bundles are to be seen. Old lady of seventy, owner of my fruit shop, describes how her house was hit, how she escaped from under the kitchen table. Assistant in grocers tells me his house is in ruins, yet they were both on the job. I think these people are wonderful.

Passed railway station after lunch on my way to the refugee committee, I have never seen anything like it. Thousands of people crowding in, cars, buses, carts and lorries, bath chairs, women pushing prams and go-karts with anything up to six or eight children trailing along, belongings in blankets, pillowcases, baskets and boxes.

Coming back from the committee at 4.00 p.m., found that the station doors had been shut. Crowds were waiting outside, mothers and children sitting on the pavement all round, constant streams of people arriving on foot and on buses, many looking exhausted. It was a heartbreaking sight.

Went up to see some friends, living on the road which leads out of town. Such an exodus, on foot, in trams, lorries, trailers, cattle floats, bicycles, delivery vans, anything that would move would be utilised. Private cars streamed past laden with women and children, with mattresses tied on top and all sorts of paraphernalia roped on behind. Hundreds were waiting at the main bus-stops. Anxiety on every face.

Nellie Bell (née Gordon)
Donaghcloney, County Down

There was quite an exodus from Belfast after that night and Bob said we were going too, to his Uncle Tom in Donaghcloney and off we went. That was a terrible time for me. Here I was, a new bride and Uncle Tom showed us an old cottage with a mud floor and said when we got our furniture down it would be as snug as a bug etc. I was terrified but said nothing ... There was definitely no room at Uncle Tom's so he took us to a friend of his, and Bob and me lived with the people in their home and Pop too. Now father was in the same room as us! ... then he and Bob trying to get to the shipyard from there was awful. After a week or so Pop said he was going to Ballymena; at least he'd get a train without walking about five miles to get it. We never moved into the cottage though our furniture was stored there.

The next four or five weeks were unbelievable, when I think of them I don't know whether to laugh or cry. Bob and me had the room to ourselves but the girl of the house had a baby and to get to her room she had to go through ours ... The baby needed a lot of attention!

Major Seán O'Sullivan
Air Raid Precautions observer from Dublin

From the morning of the 16th and all throughout the day there was a continuous 'trek' to railway stations. The refugees looked dazed and horror-stricken and many had neglected to bring more than a few belongings – I saw one man with just an extra pair of socks stuck in his pocket. Any and every means of exit from the city was availed of and the final destination appeared to be a matter of indifference.

Train after train and bus after bus were filled with those

Evacuees at the railway station, April/May 1941.

next in line. At nightfall the Northern Counties Station [in York Street] was packed from platform gates to entrance gates and still refugees were coming along in a steady stream from the surrounding streets ... Open military lorries were finally put into service and even expectant mothers and mothers with young children were put into these in the rather heavy drizzle that lasted throughout the evening.

On the 17th I heard that hundreds who either could not get away or could not leave for other reasons simply went out into the fields and remained in the open all night with whatever they could take in the way of covering.

J.C. Beckett
Lisburn, County Antrim
16 April 1941

Last night NI had another and much heavier raid. I knew nothing of it till this morning. The alert went up at 10.45; I went to bed about half an hour later, and was soon asleep. I had heard planes flying round fairly low, but there was nothing to indicate that they were hostile, and I heard no gun-fire or bombs. The rest of the family hadn't gone to bed and got no sleep till the early hours of this morning. I must sleep even more soundly than I thought ...

[The] exodus from the city is fairly general. Everywhere are cars crammed with bedding and clothes, buses and trains are crowded and I even saw families trekking off to the country on foot. When I was in town I saw no damage whatever. But Nellie, who was near York Street and Donegall Street says that in that area a lot of harm has been done and most of the rumours agree that the Antrim Rd area has been badly hit ...

I heard nothing of the raid, and so cannot say whether or not I should have been afraid. At present I have no sensation of fear, and would cheerfully go to spend tonight in any part of Belfast; how I should behave while there is another matter.

Robert Greacen
Stranmillis Road, south Belfast
16 April 1941

Dear Roy [McFadden]

Ah Der Blitz! I hope that you and the family are well, and that the windows have not been shattered. Only a few incendaries in this district. I saw some of the Antrim Road today, when I had mixed emotions. Now that it has happened the Government must be made to make decent provision for the people who have suffered.

I could have wept to see poor (in both senses) people limping over the debris with their mattress and few tattered parcels. But I am in tears when I should be saying that our people can 'take it' – as they undoubtedly can ... I must say, though, that the flares the Germans used were really beautiful. A gigantic fireworks display, thrills, excitement, relatives all-a-tremble. Fear for them and for myself: but not the fear I had in the first raid when my stomach seemed to be caving in.

What a bloody world! Sure, we can take it. I don't think I want to write about it till it's temporarily over.

Alfred Ambrose
Senior air-raid warden
Whitewell Road, north Belfast

All through that long day there was a constant stream of traffic coming down Serpentine Road (the Antrim Road was blocked near Ben Madigan Park) and up Whitewell Road to rejoin the Antrim Road further north. The police and Home Guards kept this traffic moving so as not to interfere with rescue operations or allow spectators to gather. Most of the vehicles were already full to overflowing with evacuees seeking to get into the country, but from time to time we stopped a vehicle and got scanty accommodation for some of our residents who had lost their homes.

We attended to hundreds of enquiries about all sorts of things such as billeting, evacuation, replacement of Ration Books, Identity Cards, etc, boarding-up of windows, enquiries from friends of missing and injured persons, removal of furniture, and so on. In at least one case, where a woman with small children had no man to help her, we got her house boarded up and helped her to get into the country.

The crater in Veryan Gardens was so situated in the centre of the roadway that it interfered with operations, so the military commenced shovelling the surrounding clay back into it. This clay floated on the surface of the water in the crater, and very soon this floating clay looked like a solid surface. A soldier with a rifle slung from his shoulder came along the roadway and, thinking the ground was solid, walked right into the crater. Fortunately he was an excellent swimmer, but when he commenced to swim the weight of his rifle dipped his shoulder and the rifle disappeared to the bottom of the crater which must have been some 15 feet deep. After trying in vain to recover it by surface-diving, the military procured a pump, pumped the crater dry, and the rifle was recovered.

Meanwhile the steady slogging work of turning over the debris of wrecked houses went on, and the casualty list was steadily mounting. We worked on till light began to fail, and on taking a tally, we found only one house still to be turned

Residents of Ballyclare Street, north Belfast, salvaging household effects, 15/16 April 1941.

over. Reluctantly we decided after careful examination that we had done all we could for that day and at about 23.30 hours we knocked off for a few hours' sleep.

Moya Woodside
Elmwood Avenue, south Belfast

Came home to find a message awaiting me from one of the refugees asking could I help to find somebody in the country for his wife and child. As he lived in reported Blitz area, it sounded urgent, after supper I got on my bike again and resolved to try and get through to them (they live across town about four miles away). Found that the road had only just been opened and was being policed by military. What awful scenes met me as I proceeded. It looked like photographs of Spain or China or something in the last war. Houses roofless, windowless, burnt out or burning, familiar landmarks gone and in their place vast craters and mounds of rubble. The desolation is indescribable. Thousands and thousands must be homeless, and as for the death toll, I shuddered to think of the horrors and ghastly injuries and death which have occurred.

Reached my refugees eventually to find them unharmed but terribly nervous and exhausted, Dr F said he had been through the last war on several fronts but never known such a hell as last night. Made some plans for them and tried to cheer them up.

Coming home through the gathering darkness was a horrible experience, and I admit to being rather frightened. Small parties of people were still trailing of feet towards the country (trams of course could not run on account of craters and broken wires), but no-one seemed to be returning to the city but me.

Road most of the way was inches deep in subsoil, mud thrown up from the craters, and at one point I skidded and fell flat on my face with the bike on top. A kindly policeman picked me up, and led me into a bombed house where he found some water and wiped the mud off with his handkerchief.

It was a peculiar experience to stand in someone else's scullery in the gathering darkness surrounded by debris and have a policeman direct the removal of mud from one's face. Mirrors, or course, were all shattered.

Continued my ride somewhat shaken, through more mud and passed fresh fires and crashing slates. Found two weary-eyed friends at home. We opened some wine rather than let Hitler 'have it' and drank a bottle before collapsing into bed.

BILLETING OF HOMELESS PEOPLE.

HOUSEHOLDERS ON WHOM BILLETING NOTICES ARE SERVED MUST ACCEPT PERSONS WHOM THE AUTHORITIES BILLET ON THEM.

Billeting allowances will be payable as follows:—5/— Weekly for each Adult and 3/— Weekly for each Child.

The persons billeted are expected to provide their own food. If they have no money to provide food they should apply to the nearest emergency feeding centre, about which any Air Raid Warden or Rest Centre will give information.

Persons who have lost their Ration Cards should apply at the Food Office for new Cards.

MINISTRY OF PUBLIC SECURITY.

Holy Family Parish Chronicle
Newington Avenue, north Belfast

We lost six Catholics in this parish as a result of the raid. A family Donnelly living in Hogarth St were completely wiped out. The family was mixed. The boys were Catholics and the girls non-Catholics. The body of Thomas was never got, but the other members of the family, viz. Father – James Donnelly, Robert, 23 (an invalid) and Arthur were buried in Knock graveyard. This is a graveyard containing Catholic and non-Catholic portions. The father and boys together with their mother in one grave – the three girls (sisters) and an aunt Miss McKnight were buried in the other grave. Rev. Fr Farry officiated at the burial.

Two old sisters Annie McHugh and Sarah McHugh were also killed when a land-mine came down in Halliday's Road and demolished about eleven houses including [the house] which the old sisters occupied. The bodies of the two old sisters were recovered on 19th April, identified in St George's Market and buried in Milltown Cemetery on 20th April in a special grave obtained by the parish for them.

Emma Duffin
Voluntary Aid Detachment Commandant
Stranmillis Military Hospital, south Belfast

The next day I had promised to give a First Aid lecture, one of a course of four, to a class organised by the Women's Voluntary Service at a school on the top of the Oldpark Road. I asked would I still be required and was told 'yes' to carry on. I knew the tram service was dislocated so left myself plenty of time or so I thought, but I soon realised I would be very late. Tram was crowded, chiefly with people wanting to see the damage. The centre was all right, but when I reached Royal Avenue, I saw a crater in the road and the Free Library was pitted all over, and the shop people were busy boarding up their windows on both sides of the road.

I made my way to the tram, and finally decided to hail a car. Two men responded to my appeal, and though they were going up the Antrim Road, they good-naturedly said they'd take me the whole way. They both had what looked like Government cars and so I imagined had petrol, so I accepted their offer …

We passed the Mater Hospital where many victims had been taken. The nurses' home had been hit; as we got higher up the road, we began to realize the extent of the damage. Little side streets in ruins, houses reduced to dust. We were diverted into another road, not much better. We saw a street shelter which had received a direct hit, killing most of the occupants. The concrete top seemed to have been sliced off. When I arrived at my school I felt almost a fool, to come to speak to householders here on First Aid.

Many to whom I should have spoken would now be beyond the help of First Aid themselves, but having come, I made my way into the school. It was intact, so were all its windows. It had been used for the last two days to interview applicants for relief, given temporary assistance, arrange evacuation but it was practically empty and the voluntary workers were snatching a well earned luncheon. Feeling rather foolish, I turned away. There were no trams. In spite of my welcome lift, I had walked a good way already, and my gasmask and steel helmet weighed me down, but there was nothing for it but to start for home.

Buses were running at long intervals but were so crowded, there was no hope of a seat. I was joined by a friendly little person who had been a VAD in the last war. She had gone to look for a friend but found her gone. We tramped on, and presently a woman showed us a shortcut. She told me how she and her mother, a large stout woman, had spent the night under the dining room table. Soon we reached the devastated area, not a window was left unbroken. Many homes were deserted. Glimpses down side streets showed demolition squads and military digging frantically … A church was completely gutted, yet a plate-glass window in the butcher's next to it, had not received a crack.

A policeman stopped his car, and took us as far as the nearest tram, but the trams were too full to attempt. Everywhere were people with parcels or suitcases, struggling to get away. Who shall blame them? We tramped on, and at last were offered another lift. I returned to the hospital exhausted but feeling how grateful I should be, that I and all my family and our homes were intact.

J.C. Beckett
Lisburn, County Antrim
17–18 April 1941

On Thursday I saw for the first time the damage done by the bombs and I saw more of it today. In going over reports at the R/C [Rest Centre] I found frequent refs to casualties and to corpses.

In spite of it all I am unimpressed. Anderson said to me that he felt very gloomy as a result of what he had seen and heard – perhaps he is influenced by the fact that the house in which he has his digs is in the danger area of an UXB [unexploded bomb]. My chief feeling is one of disappointment that I was out of it all. I can't blame myself for being away, and yet I feel as if I should have been there. When I see others who have done so much and had so little relief my own part seems neglible. Yet I can do so little – partly because I am already tied up with fire-watching, partly because I am so imperfectly acquainted with the routine of the R/C work.

Sir Wilfrid Spender
Head of the Northern Ireland Civil Service
17 April 1941

I thought the police arrangements were working very well, mainly due to the handling of the Inspector General himself and I think his conduct in accepting directions was admirable. He was able to concentrate his attention practically on Belfast and if he had been unable to do this owing to work throughout the whole Province I would have less confidence that the police arrangements in the city would work so satisfactorily.

Although I think the Government should emerge with credit in respect of its handling of this particular blitz attack ... I am definitely of the opinion that the present machinery would break down if we had a series of such attacks, or if there were invasion or a more general attack over Northern Ireland. There is in my view too much centralization of the Government's functions in the Ministry of Public Security and I think that the Ministry should be relieved of some of the work which it is undertaking on behalf of the Government as a whole, letting it concentrate mainly on its own particular functions.

Moya Woodside
Elmwood Avenue, south Belfast
17 April 1941

It has now been discovered that what we had was as severe as Coventry or Glasgow. Hundreds of planes were used. Everyone I meet has some terrible story of death and damage and disorganisation. Electricity and water still okay but gas off. I spent half the morning running around trying to boil water on picnic outfits, and ancient spirit burners resuscitated from the attic, called in a plumber to see if the oven on our ancient (coal) range could be made workable.

Rang up gas works to order some coke, and the clerk started telling about his experiences as a warden and about dead bodies. He said among other things that the many soldiers about were swearing in their impotence 'if we could only get at them' was being heard on all sides. This raiding only seems to make people more bitter and determined than ever. I myself begin to feel that I should have tried to add some WVS [Women's Voluntary Service] work to my already over-crowded life.

My mother telephones to say that she took eight evacuees last night, two mothers and six children. Says one mother is about to have another baby any minute, but they are all filthy, the smell in the room is terrible, they refuse all food except bread and tea, the children have made puddles all over the floor etc. She is terribly sorry for them and kindliness itself but finds this revelation of how the other half live rather overpowering.

I feel so restless and can't settle down to anything. Cooking is a problem, one doesn't know what to plan or arrange when the gas may be on this evening or perhaps on at half-strength.

Went up to see my mother who is now discovered to her horror that several of the evacuee children are TB, and two have skin diseases on their heads.

Evacuation is taking on panic proportions. Roads out of town are still one stream of cars, with mattresses and bedding tied on top. Everything on wheels is being pressed into service. People are leaving from all parts of town and not only from the bombed areas. Where they are going or what they will find even when they get there, nobody knows. This business presents a problem of a first proportion to Stormont. Belfast is the only large town in Ulster, most of the country towns have also been bombed, and there is absolutely no provision for the reception and feeding of those vast numbers.

Alfred Ambrose
Senior air-raid warden
Whitewell Road, north Belfast

During Thursday and Friday Demolition Squads arrived and commenced taking down those damaged houses which were considered to be dangerous. Keeping a house or two ahead of the Demolition Squads, the Wardens hastily carried out the furniture and other contents of the condemned houses and placed these chattels in neat piles, opposite the house from which they had been taken. We had, however, no means of putting identity marks on the contents of each house, and when the Furniture Salvage Vans arrived, we saw our salvage efforts largely brought to nought, as the contents of several houses were mixed together in one van in such a manner that we felt they could never be sorted out again …

On Friday a stocktaking was made of all persons who were known to have been in the damage area during the raid. This proved a very difficult task. We dealt with the problem household by household, and all available Wardens pooled their information. Many people went away from their homes without informing the Wardens, though there were isolated cases where people went to some trouble to send messages to us to inform us that they or certain members of their families were safe. After sending scouts around the hospitals and checking the names of missing people with the lists of casualties published at the City Hall, we eventually reached the stage where the Senior Warden was satisfied that all were accounted for, except one small boy of whom we had no news

Queen's University students assist the demolition squads on Eglinton Street.

whatever. Next day a paragraph appeared in the local press stating that an unidentified child had been found sleeping on a seat in one of the hospitals. It proved to be the child about which we had been worrying.

Air Raid Precautions Report *
18 April 1941

The morale was very high. All services worked themselves to a standstill.

AFS [Auxiliary Fire Service]
The entire personnel was called out and carried on through the night and most of the next day.

Casualty
All personnel were in action, together with reliefs from regions and worked wonderfully under most trying conditions. *Lessons learned.* Ambulances must be increased by 50%, second line First Aid Posts must be obtained – 5% ambulances became ineffective through enemy action and owing to other various causes.

Wardens
Reporting magnificent, became 'jack of all trades' and shepherded public. Wardens from unaffected districts went to affected districts to help. Every job was, and is still being done without one word of quibble.

---

* Reports would have been prepared for a range of military and civil authorities but ultimately for the Minister of Public Security, John MacDermott. As was the custom of the time, most of these reports were very short – usually only one page in length – and unsigned.

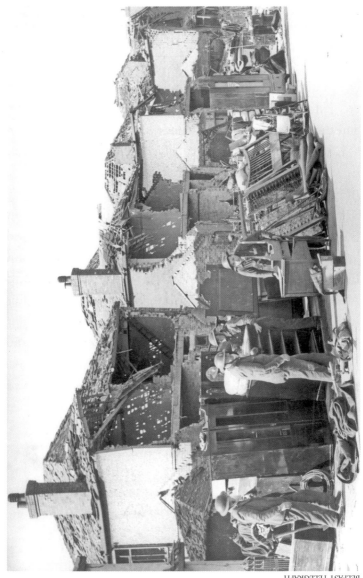

Furniture being removed from houses, Sunningdale Park, north Belfast.

Moya Woodside
Elmwood Avenue, south Belfast
18 April 1941

Only now three days afterwards are people beginning to realise the results of the raid. Paper is full of cancellations, notices of changes of addresses, lists of names under 'by enemy action' in obituary columns, instructions to homeless, etc. Unidentified bodies have been collected at the market and there is talk of a mass funeral ...

Everyone is quoting Lord Haw-Haw! He said this or he said that. He will give us time to bury the dead before the next attack. Tuesday was only a sample. People living in such and such a district will have their turn. The harbour is entirely destroyed, and so on. How much is truth, and how much is colourful and panic imagination I'm not in a position to say. No-one I asked had actually heard Haw-Haw say these things himself, it was always 'they say'.

Left my shopping to rather late in the afternoon and found there was no bread left and hardly any biscuits.

Wilton was a funeral home in north Belfast.

Evacuation still going on. Further phone conversations with mother re: her evacuees. A grandfather and two more children have turned up last night making a grand total of eleven. None of them went to bed until 12.30 p.m. Today she made for their dinner a sausage pie (it was very nice) and a milk pudding. Both were sent back to the kitchen, messed about and not eaten 'they don't like this sort of food, when are we going to have our tea, we don't want that jam you gave us yesterday'. All these eleven people were being fed by my mother and at her expense and from her own supplies and this was all the thanks she got.

Robert Greacen
19 April 1941

Dear Roy,

I had no reply to my last letter, asking whether or not you had 'weathered' the Blitz so, having been told of the alarming state of Knutsford Drive I went up today to see what had happened. Your father was there packing up (I expect he told you I called) and I'm afraid I wasn't able to help him much.

If I hadn't seen some of the bombed areas I would say that you were unfortunate in having the windows smashed in and the house shaken. Instead, I must say that – living in the Cliftonville district – your family was lucky to escape injury, that feeling doesn't lessen the inconvenience of the raid.

I hear that since the attack I – whose home suffered no injury whatever – have had lots of inconvenience one way and another. The worst thing of all has been the irregularity of my feeding. But then I have succumbed to prolonged indigestion. I find it difficult to believe that all this terror and misery and destruction has swept across the face of our reasonably (and comparatively) beautiful city, so that my judgement of the whole thing must be deferred. Not that I have changed my views, but I will say this, commonplace as it is: Hitler won't win by destroying our homes.

PC Herbie Ross
Glenravel Street RUC Station

As dead bodies were being recovered they were brought to a few places in the city in order to facilitate relatives in identification. The largest place was the Markets. A team of men nearby made rough type coffins mainly nailing planks together and a body was laid therein. Human remains were in bags and labelled as such.

I was on duty in the Markets, allowing a certain number of people to enter one at a time as they were arriving in numbers wanting to know if any of the dead were their relations. As they waited for entry, they were not talking or weeping. They appeared to be suffering from shock.

I remember a sailor who arrived at Belfast that morning and, on his arrival at home on the Antrim Road, found it was

NORTHERN WHIG

BELFAST
CIVIL DEFENCE AUTHORITY

THE BODIES OF UNIDENTIFIED VICTIMS OF THE RECENT AIR RAID may be seen by relatives in ST. GEORGE'S MARKET on FRIDAY, 18th APRIL, from 3 p.m. until 7 p.m., and on SATURDAY, from 9 a.m. until 7 p.m.

Unidentified and unclaimed bodies will be buried by the above authority in the reserved ground at the City Cemetery on MONDAY, 21st instant, leaving the above Market at 12 noon.

17th April, 1941.

completely demolished and then came back to the Markets to find out if his father, mother and two other members of his family were among the dead. He [had been] in and out on three occasions and said to me he had had no 'luck' as he could only find two brothers in boxes ... I asked him if he had any more 'luck' this time and he replied that he was lucky in that he was [now] able to identify all his family and said he wished to God that he had been there in a box with them. After people had identified their dead relatives they then showed their distress.

Emma Duffin
Voluntary Aid Detachment Commandant
Stranmillis Military Hospital, south Belfast

Saturday afternoon, the fifth day after the Blitz I went to the Market [St George's Market]. Will I ever bring myself to buy flowers and vegetables there again?

The gates were guarded by police, but at sight of my uniform they opened them. Molly, poor thing, had already been there and, to a certain extent prepared me for what I was to see. The place was full of coffins, some varnished but the majority plain ...

At the end of the hall was a Salvation Army Mobile Canteen, and beside it was a rough table where some men with papers took particulars. Red Cross and St John nurses and some civilian volunteers met and went round with relatives, two men went round with each group and opened the coffins, lifting the lids. There were two doctors in attendance. A man watered the ground with disinfectant from a watering pot, a wise precaution as the place smelt.

It was a lofty airy place fortunately but a bitter cold wind whistled through the gates, and the disinfectant had soaked and made puddles on the floor. It was a hideous nightmare.

Only small groups were allowed in at a time, mercifully. I went with a man and his wife first. They looked desolate, exhausted with red rimmed eyes, and haggard faces. They were looking for a sister-in-law. They had seen all these coffins but more were being brought in and they hung around waiting. I found a Mrs Lindsay, a St John member and she and I went round with another group. There was a certain amount of organisation, the men's coffins were together, and the women's and children's at the other side of the hall. As each was identified, it was our duty to put the names of the body and the identifier in the coffin, and men moved it to the side, where they were put till the relatives removed them for burial. Particulars were handed to the men at the desks. In some of the coffins rough notes were written in chalk. The name of the street where the body had been found, a rough description 'middle-aged woman grey hair', 'young girl dark hair', 'young girl wearing necklace' ... All the way to the place I had told myself I was bound to see horrible sights, but only when seen could the full horror be realised.

I had seen many dead, but they had died in hospital beds, their eyes had been reverently closed, their hands crossed in their breasts, death had to a certain extent been glossed over, made decent. It was solemn, tragic, dignified, but here it was grotesque, repulsive, horrible. No attendant nurse has soothed the last moments of these victims, no gentle reverent hands had closed those eyes, nor crossed these arms. With tangled hair, staring eyes, clutching hands, contorted limbs, their grey-green faces covered with dirt, they lay, bundled into the coffins, half shrouded in rugs or blankets or an occasional sheet, still wearing their dirty, torn twisted garments. Death should be dignified, peaceful. Hitler had made even death grotesque!

I felt outraged. I should have felt pity, sympathy, grief, but instead feelings of repulsion and disgust assailed me. The men who were moving the coffins by means of dirty strips of calico slipped beneath them, were of the roughest, coarsest type. One was disfigured by a skin disease. They shouted to each other as they worked. God knows it was a distasteful enough job and they had been at it for five days, enough to stifle feelings in more sensitive people. A youngish girl stood in a group dressed in Red Cross uniform. She was chewing sweets. 'We've been on since 9.30 this morning, it's an awful job, we're just about fed up' she said in a common voice. I was sorry for her but shuddered to think of grieving relatives searching amongst those gruesome remains for someone they loved, being accompanied by a girl of that type. It was no job for a girl and nobody should have been kept at it for more than a few hours at a time.

Mrs Lindsay and I found to our horror a child about seven or eight seated on a chair, waiting for her mother. How anyone could have allowed a child to enter that Hall of Death I do not know. Mercifully someone had set her behind a screen, but she could not but have seen the coffins when she entered, and she must have known the terrible errand that had brought her mother there. What impression would she carry through life of that day?

We got her some tea, a bun, and biscuits from the Salvation Army Canteen and left her there, though the thought of anybody eating in that place filled me with nausea. One group of people consisting of six relatives seemed to be touring the lines of coffins over and over again.

One of the girls, of a very low looking type, had lost a brother and was looking for another relative, beside her a strange, repulsive creature shuffled, her shabby hat perched on the very top of her head, her twisted hands clasped in front of her. She mumbled and murmured words I could not catch, retelling horrors and, I could not help feeling, perhaps unjustly, enjoying a certain amount of satisfaction from being included in the drama and tragedy.

The woman was looking in vain for her mother and sister; she had been up from the country on this awful quest three days running. She was wrapped in a shawl and her husband looked a rough type, but her brother who had just arrived from Dublin, hoping to carry his mother and sister off to safety and had instead been brought here to search for their bodies, was very well dressed in a good pilot overcoat and soft hat. He was in a terrible state ... I wanted to get him a hot drink, but found the Mobile Canteen gone. I asked a policeman where there was a restaurant, but he said they were closed round here as they'd run out of food after the Blitz.

My two hours duty drew to an end. The place was closing down till the next day, Sunday, the last day. After that any unclaimed bodies were to be buried in a common grave.

I came away, drawing deep breaths of fresh air. So this was the result of a Blitz, I had heard of it, pictured it, now seen it. I prayed I should never see it again. I saw in my mind's eye the grey-green faces of children, one in a coffin with its mother, and the bare foot of a little child and I heard the voice of a woman in my ear, asking for a child, a little boy in 'velvet trousers'. I tried not to think of it, and think of 'whatsoever things are good, whatsoever things are lovely, whatsoever things are of good report': birds, flowers, beautiful skies and seas. Hitler could not distort those.

Moya Woodside
Elmwood Avenue, south Belfast
19 April 1941

A man called to collect payment for some coke delivered to me yesterday and told me I was extremely lucky to have got it at all. 'Bakeries are working twenty-four hours a day', he said, 'and we have our work cut out to keep them going.' The only thing the Government has to feed the people on is tea and bread.

Official appeal in the paper for those whose houses are undamaged to remain in them or return to them. The countryside has apparently been besieged and whole areas of town left deserted.

More about my mother's evacuees. She has now been reduced to four and has discovered that this particular woman's house is quite habitable but she does not seem to have any intention to return to it. 'My nerves are too bad,' she complained, just sits all day in the midst of dirt and untidiness drinking innumerable cups of tea!

BELFAST AIR RAID:
Official Notices

The following notices are issued by the Ministry of Public Security, Northern Ireland, and the Belfast Civil Defence Authority:—

(1) Accommodation for the Homeless.

Arrangements are being made by the authorities to billet homeless people as quickly as possible.

It is the imperative duty of householders to receive the homeless into their houses. The authorities will take a serious view of any refusal to do so.

(2) Stay at Home if you can.

People whose homes are still habitable should continue to live in them, and so relieve the pressure on the authorities, who are fully engaged in providing accommodation and transport for those whose homes have been destroyed.

17th April, 1941.

NORTHERN WHIG

Lieutenant G.G. Ryan
Irish Army
To G2, Irish Military Intelligence

On Saturday 19th April, while in the company of some people from the Six Counties, which included a Captain C., Inniskillings, stationed in Armagh, and another young officer,

I learned that the reaction in the North to the sending up of the Fire Brigades is tremendous and in these people's words 'has done more good than fifty year's talk'.

They, while coming down South on holiday, travelled with evacuees and commented in terms of the greatest enthusiasm on the reception given them at the various stations en route. The whole party seemed to be delighted with their freedom of movement and with the opportunities which Dublin afforded them of eating and drinking and to more or less envy us down here.

Fred Bashford
Headquarters, British Troops Northern Ireland
Belvoir Park, south Belfast
20 April 1940

As you probably read we had a super *blitz* last week. Not that I saw much of the actual raid, but the repercussions were pretty violent. Scenes witnessed here duplicated those seen in a dozen different towns lately – ruined streets, derelict houses, mourning people. And the refugees! Is there anything more pitiable in the world than this aimless trekking from a bombed area??

Carts, prams, motor-cyle combinations – all piled high with human and material flotsam – trudging feet, crying children, the despair graved on faces, the abject fear of a further blow ... what a picture for civilisation to snap for its altruism.

I think Ulster thought itself immune from this sort of thing – the blow struck very hard when it did come. No doubt there will be more but I'm sure there'll be stronger wills to bear them and that they have been braced by the worst there is.

Moya Woodside
Elmwood Avenue, south Belfast
20 April 1941

Drove to a small country town thirty miles away [Ballymena] to visit in-laws. All the way there we kept passing lorries and cars piled high with bedding and furniture and the same coming back in the afternoon. Sister-in-law, WVS member, tells of the appalling influx from the slums the day after the raid. They were totally unprepared for such numbers, and for the type of people arriving.

The whole town is horrified by the filth of these evacuees, and by their dirty habits and their take-it-for-granted attitude. Belfast slums dwellers are pretty far down and to those not used to seeing poverty and misery at close quarters the effect is over-whelming. 'The smell is terrible,' says my sister-in-law. They don't even use the lavatory they just do it on the floor, grown-ups and children. 'Our blankets in two nights have been absolutely ruined.' She said she had been given the job of finding billets for the evacuees and was ashamed to have to ask decent working people with clean houses to take in such guests. More are 'scared out' than 'bombed out', too.

I believe it is the same all over the countryside. At least it may do good in one way, if it makes people think about housing and homes in the slums. Complacency and/or ignorance has been rudely shattered these last few days. 'We can see now why you're so keen on your birth-control clinic,' my sister-in-law remarked. I felt quite cheered.

The OWL, Belfast Royal Academy School Magazine
Editorial
Summer 1941

The air raids have caused a considerable exodus from Belfast, especially from those districts that suffered most. This has reduced the numbers of our various departments. In the upper part of the school the attendance is very good but there is a marked falling off in the lower forms. In these circumstances the Headmaster, with the energetic support of the preparatory and kindergarten staff has been able to establish branch schools in the places to which our junior pupils have been chiefly evacuated.

Four such branches have been started: at the Roader, Portrush, under Miss W.G. Salters; at Ballygally, under Miss Houston; at Shore Street Presbyterian Church Hall, Donaghadee, under Miss Elsie Salters; and at Coolnafranky, Cookstown, under Miss Bass.

The parents of our exiled junior pupils have cordially welcomed these ventures and we believe these branch schools will prove of very great value in maintaining the educational efficiency of the Academy.

Holy Family Parish Chronicle
Newington Avenue, north Belfast
June 1941

The evacuation of people from the parish following the air raid was heart rending and for almost two months, not a single child was present at the schools. The teachers were assigned to various schools in the country – only the two principal teachers remained Mr A Donnelly and Miss Nora Collins.

1941 Register of Crimes, County of Belfast
Belfast B District (Hastings Street)
21 April 1941, 1 p.m.

John F., 11 Wigton St, Labourer, was caught stealing articles from the house of Mrs Jane McQ. which had been bombed.

At Custody Court on 22.04.1941 he pleaded guilty and was sentenced to six months imprisonment and hard labour.

Sergeant G.A. (Bertie) McGarvey
RAF Yatesbury, Calne, Wiltshire

I'm afraid the family didn't come off too well in the first blitz on Belfast. One of the bombs wrecked the house completely but fortunately no-one was injured. Each of them seems to have had a lucky escape. Grandad had for some reason or another stayed up a little longer than usual that night and just after he normally would have been in bed the ceiling came down on his bed.

Mita, too, had a very lucky break. She had heard what she thought was a plane crashing in the road outside so went into the drawing room to investigate it (talk about nerve!) She went to the window to look out and some-one called her so she turned around and took a couple of steps towards the door. No sooner had she done so than there was a crash and the window landed in fragments on the spot where she had been standing! They are now all safe at Lurgan at Aunty Jennie's place.

In the house opposite there were five people killed, including a four month's old baby. Roy carried most of the bodies out and seems to have had some experiences he's not likely to forget. It certainly looks as if Ireland is not such a safe place after all!

Doreen Bates
Tax Inspector
Sydenham, east Belfast
20 April 1941

A fine sunny day. Sundays here so far have been good no matter how bad weekdays have been. I went for a walk ... and was stopped by a local Home Guard and asked for my identity card, where I was going and why. When I said 'home to lunch' he seems a little dashed. At 1.00 I heard in the news that London had had another bad raid – I hadn't heard from the family after the Wednesday raid. It is hideous being so remote.

Moya Woodside
Elmwood Avenue, south Belfast
21 April 1941

Working as usual at Welfare Office which is also Citizens Advice Bureau. We dealt with a stream of people asking all the questions (too varied to enumerate here) which inevitably arrives after a raid. It was noticeable that those who are unhurt and whose houses were undamaged were much more difficult to handle than those who had actually suffered. I don't believe the general public yet has an idea of the extent of the damage. Whole streets of working class houses are simply no more. The authorities were quite unprepared to deal with such thousands and thousands of homeless and the disorganisation is dreadful ...

Duke and Duchess of Gloucester have been hastily imported to tour the bombed areas and (presumably) fortify morale. People are beginning to trickle back, as the word has gone around that empty and undamaged houses will be taken over for the homeless. My mother's bunch left this evening on

CITY AND COUNTY BOROUGH OF BELFAST

OWNERS OR TENANTS OF HOUSES DAMAGED, which can be rendered habitable without extensive repairs, should, if practicable, carry out these repairs themselves. Where necessary materials are not available householders can obtain limited quantities by applying to the undermentioned firms and producing certificates from their district wardens that damage capable of simple temporary repair has been sustained. While every effort is being made to have repairs carried out by builders, it is essential in the public interest as well as in their own and that of their families that those who can should help themselves.

The following suppliers have been authorised by the Belfast Corporation to supply materials at the expense of the Corporation, on production of the above certificate:—

TIMBER—J. P. CORRY & CO., LTD., Corporation Street.
ULSTER TIMBER COY., Duncrue Street.
LYTLE & POLLOCK, LTD., 18, Duncrue Street.

FELT— DAVID ANDERSON & SON, LTD., 62, Short Strand.
JOS. BLAIR, LTD., Church Lane.
ERSKINE FELT WORKS, Greencastle.
D. R. MARTIN & SONS, Castleton Gardens.
VULCANITE, LTD., Stranmillis.
J. ROGERS, LTD., 68, Victoria Street.
N. MacNAUGHTON & SONS, LTD., Corporation Street.

CITY AND COUNTY BOROUGH OF BELFAST

URGENT NOTICE

Any builder free to undertake first aid repairs and make dwelling houses reasonably habitable to communicate at once with Mr. Wilshere, Education Architect, Old Town Hall.

R. B. DONALD, City Surveyor.

this account, 'she was beginning to get bored anyway', but the children didn't want to go.

Northern Whig
22 April 1941

While demolition squads toiled to wipe away grim reminders of Wednesday's attack on Belfast, the unknown and unclaimed victims of the raid were buried yesterday. The hearses were military lorries. Captain Martelli represented the Governor, and representatives of the Prime Minister and members of the Cabinet, the Lord Mayor and Corporation, with representatives of the Civil Defence and military authorities, followed the cortege.

Inside St George's Market, where victims awaited identification, the Bishop of Down and Connor and Dromore, the Moderator of the General Assembly, Rabbi Shachter, Bishop Mageean, and representatives of other Churches performed the last funeral rites. Thence the bodies were taken to the City and Milltown Cemeteries …

Women knelt in the thronged streets near the market and prayed as the procession passed. Soldiers, sailors, airmen, members of the Civil Defence Services, and police saluted, while blinds were drawn and flags at half mast.

Along the route to the cemeteries traffic was hushed, and housewives stood at their doorsteps in silent sympathy. The cortege passed heaps of rubble – all that remained of many of the victims' homes. Where children had played, soldiers and civilians rested from their labours, and with shovel or pick in hand stood to attention.

On the front and sides of each lorry were wreaths from the Government, Corporation, Civil Defence and fighting services, and many from anonymous sympathizers.

Large crowds gathered at the cemeteries, among them a soldier on leave whose home was wrecked. He does not know whether his wife and four children have been killed or saved.

T.J. Campbell, MP
House of Commons, Stormont
22 April 1941

Death during this past week has taken its toll from the houses of the well-to-do in Belfast, and a far fuller toll from the homes in the narrow streets where life crowds thick and where the struggle for existence never ends from the cradle to the grave. Those streets are to-day streets of sorrow. Some have become the hecatombs of innocent and helpless victims of this cruel blast of war – swept into eternity in the twinkling of an eye.

We reverence and mourn for those who have gone, and in all sincerity, speaking on behalf of every member of this community, we tender our sympathy to those who will long miss them. We sorrow and we suffer also with the living who have been hurt or who have been damaged in worldly goods. We have gratitude deep and deserved for the devoted workers and volunteers who during those fierce, dark hours when death was hovering over part of Belfast and who day and night since then have been facing extreme peril to serve and succour their fellow-beings. The men worked heroically; the women were no less heroic. (Hon. Members: Hear, hear.)

This last week has been a very grim testing time for our citizens, but they have bethought themselves during that trying period how they could help their neighbours. Amid their agony and tribulation a fine civic spirit, a rich comradeship, a true understanding among the people have shone with brightness.

There have been manifestations of goodwill and practical generosity and sympathy from across the Border, and we should not conclude to-day without an expression of our earnest and grateful acknowledgment of those manifestations. One touch of nature makes the whole world kin.

John MacDermott
Minister of Public Security
House of Commons, Stormont
22 April 1941

The mighty task of coping with the vast tide of suffering and distress was shouldered by the welfare services, assisted by many men and women of good-will throughout the country. The magnitude of this task is hard to describe and difficult to estimate in advance, but some idea of what was accomplished may be gathered from the following approximate figures for meals supplied under the emergency feeding arrangements which had been made by the Civil Defence Authority in Belfast.

On Wednesday, the 16th, it is estimated that 70,000 meals were supplied. On the following day, Thursday, the estimate is 60,000. On Friday the number was between 40,000 and 50,000; Saturday between 30,000 and 40,000; Sunday, 20,000, and yesterday some 10,000.

The question of the homeless and distressed is still with us, but plans are being formed to meet the future in the light of the experience so recently gained, and with the realisation that the aftermath of the battle raises problems as difficult and as important as those which the battle itself presents. In this connection I should like to pay tribute to the emergency arrangements made by many local authorities outside the borough of Belfast in dealing with those who were billeted upon them at very short notice, and to the kindness of the people who, on many occasions, did not wait on any formal arrangements.

Moya Woodside
Elmwood Avenue, south Belfast
23 April 1941

Published death toll (provisional) is 500, seriously injured 420, other injuries over 1,000. Death toll will be higher as in some districts they are still digging bodies out. A friend of mine had it from the lips of the minister of Public Security himself that he sent to England the day after the raid for two evacuees experts. These men duly arrived by air but, 'were helpless, couldn't advise anything'. The panic rush from town was such that they had never seen anything like it.

It's extraordinary how life goes on almost normally in other parts of the town. I went to a sherry party this evening given by the staff of one of our military hospitals, and there we all were, drinking, nibbling delicacies, chattering and laughing as if no such horror had ever occurred. At this gathering we 'native Irish' were in a small minority the most of those present being English medical men and their expatriated wives.

Doreen Bates
Tax Inspector
Sydenham, east Belfast
24 April 1941

Rumours still float about concerning casualties. The official figure is 500+ killed; I heard from Mrs B., purporting to come from ARP [Air Raid Precautions] control, that there were over 1000. I have also heard … over 2000.

Casualty Bureau, Belfast City Hall
24 April 1941

Regarding the unidentified ... in very many cases the information furnished to the Bureau was too meagre to be of any assistance to persons wishing to identify remains. It appeared that the private mortuaries had not staff in attendance capable of dealing with these forms.

Complaints of an even more serious nature were made by enquirers viz. that bodies which has been identified by them in a certain mortuary were removed to another while the relatives were away making arrangements for burial. This last occurrence caused considerable distress to relatives of the killed, and it appears to me that steps should be taken to provide against a recurrence.

Moya Woodside
Elmwood Avenue, south Belfast
26 April 1941

Saw various adults and children walking about in clothes obviously of American origin. The effect is sometimes surprising! Heard more stories of evacuees dirt, behaviour and ingratitude. Some hostess insisted on a bath but the results were apparently ineffective. Bed wetting and skin disease among children the most commonest complaint. Vermin accepted as an inevitability. Those who aroused the most indignation were the 'scared out', who took up accommodation meant for genuinely homeless and refused to return to their own houses.

27 April 1941

People are still leaving town, every day one hears of fresh removals. Yesterday driving to seaside town sixty miles away we continually passed lorries laden with bedding, furniture (anyone who owned a lorry must have made their fortune this past fortnight.)

Papers are full of advertisements of houses, and flats in town to let, balanced by an equally large number of ads for houses and rooms to let in the country. It is really astonishing! Raid – Raid – Raid – how sick I am of hearing it. No other subject of conversation exists. At customary family gathering today it went on and on, being discussed from every angle, each newcomer contributing something fresh, till I reached the stage of feeling I should scream.

We had an 'alert' on Thursday night, followed by gunfire, which went on for some time. Lots of people took their cars and drove out into the country to wait for the All Clear. An aunt of mine, who thus transported two maids and a dog, said that the particular spot where she went (almost a mile beyond the city boundary) was crowded with cars; and some were even camping out in tents.

28 April 1941

At Welfare office we had two cases of bedridden old ladies wishing to be evacuated – *and nothing can be done for them.* The government have no made provision for this type of case, and the Infirmary (Poor Law) refuses to take them in, alleging shortage of beds and nurses. They will only accept the *homeless* infirm. So we have to tell people that if they wait until they are bombed, then we can help them.

One of the old women in question this morning is 75, paralysed, and without the power of speech. She is still lying in the room where the windows and doors were blown in on top of her and was helpless when it happened to even to summon her niece who was sheltering below stairs. Eugenically speaking, of course, such people would be better dead: but their anguish of mind must be dreadful.

Spent a lugubrious half hour putting some papers (bank books, account and address books) in a suitcase, ready to be removed in the event of a time bomb. Can't make up my mind what to do about my clothes. Some people have packed suitcases deposited in different parts of the town; but so far I cannot bring myself to do this. The whole thing is a gamble anyway. Mentally, I am torn between the wish to go on leading a life as normal as possible, and the wish to have something left from the wreck – if it comes.

I suppose people in much bombed areas of England have found their own solution to this problem long ago.

30 April 1941

Out on Welfare case work in the blitzed areas. I had five families to visit and found one burnt out and departed, whereabouts unknown, three others also gone from houses, uninhabitable though still standing; and the fifth evacuated from an undamaged house. It was a scene of desolation: whole streets of roofless and windowless houses, with an occasional notice chalked on the doors 'Gone to Ballymena' or some other country address.

Not a soul about, except demolition workers. Enormous gaps or mounds of bricks where previously some familiar building had stood. More than a fortnight now since the raid, yet it still looks raw and obscene. People who survived that night of horror there will surely never be the same again. Easy to understand why even habitable houses are deserted.

BELFAST AIR RAID EMERGENCY.

If **you** have changed your address since Monday please send a post card to Casualty Enquiries Bureau, City Hall, Belfast. Your friends are anxious to know your whereabouts.

Issued by the Belfast Civil Defence Authority.

17th April, 1941.

Julia Walsh
Teacher, St Dominic's Grammar School, Falls Road
Writing from Westport, County Mayo
1 May 1941

Dear Mother Columba,
I was waiting to hear from you before sending in my letter of resignation to the Governing Body. I could not possibly face the strain of a further term in Belfast under present war conditions and after much consideration, I have decided not to return there ...

I shall always remember your unfailing kindness and consideration to me during your term as Head Mistress.

Moya Woodside
Elmwood Avenue, south Belfast
2 May 1941

At weekly Welfare committee we only had seven cases, instead of our usual number of twenty-five to thirty. The type of family we deal with is largely bombed out or evacuated, and work since the raid has been 50% relief and 95% advising.

3 May 1941

Met wife of organist and music teacher, looking weary and harassed. She told me that since the raid they had gone to live in two rooms in a small town twelve miles away, as her husband 'couldn't stand' the strain (their home is in a quite undamaged area). 'It's awful what it costs,' she said, 'All four of us have to travel every day and pay for two hours and John lost all his pupils on the _____Rd (mentioning bombed district) and the trains and trams are so crowded – you've no idea.' Her experience and situation is common. Everyone one hears remarks 'oh, I'm living out at so and so now' or 'I have to get up at six to be in time at the office' etc. The strain thrown on the transport facilities by all those unaccustomed commuters is terrific. Three or four buses run where previously one sufficed, and buses have evidently been borrowed from Dublin, Glasgow and even Sheffield, judging from the licence plates.

I believe that the railway stations at night are like a football match. Numbers of people, especially the lower paid workers, must find it impossible to manage when railway or bus season tickets are suddenly added to their expenses. Then too, if travel to and from work takes perhaps an hour or 1½ hours instead of 15 mins, and with maybe billets instead of a house, discontent and weariness is bound to be manifest.

The
May Raid

Belfast had been convulsed by the April bombing raids. The annihilation of entire families, the destruction of entire streets and, in particular, the mass funerals of unknown victims made it painfully apparent how vulnerable the city actually was. All anyone wanted to know was would it happen again?

After Easter Tuesday, troops had been used for debris clearance and salvage work, a task that everywhere else in the UK was undertaken by civilians. While the appearance of the military in the city boosted morale in some quarters, military chiefs were deeply alarmed at how much was being asked of them and their men.

The Army Commander of the Belfast Area, in an official report compiled after the Easter Tuesday raid, asserted that he was keen to make full use of what he called 'my military assets' – presumably men and equipment – but pointed out that in order to do so it was best to deal with a single authority. But that did not exist in Belfast. The chief Air Raid Precautions officers handled air raid precautions, and first aid and rescue services; the Auxiliary Fire Service (AFS) was independent; evacuation was a government affair; road clearances and so on were a matter for the Emergency Repairs Committee; and bomb disposal priorities were laid down by the government.

But even worse than the confusion caused in the aftermath of the April raids by the absence of any coordinating authority was the failure at both Stormont and City Hall to make adequate provision for the possibility of a further air raid. Senior military officers in their reports (submitted to the Ministry of Public Security) identified a lack of drive and determination in recruiting and training wardens, fire-fighting personnel and in the preparation for the serious refugee problem that would result from more bombing raids.

On the night of Sunday 4 May 1941, the German bombers returned, and with near perfect visibility, found it easy to score even more direct hits, targeting the harbour, shipyards and Shorts aircraft factory as well as the city centre.

It is believed that close to 100,000 tons of incendiary bombs were dropped in less than four hours, creating fires on a scale not seen during any of the previous raids. There were reports that the fires, especially those in the docks district which was totally ablaze, could even be seen on the Glenshane Pass, almost fifty miles away. The official German report on this raid, quoted by John Blake in his official history of Northern Ireland in the Second World War, concluded that 'in view of the ideal bombing conditions and the large conflagrations observed, the raid can be considered a success'. But because large numbers had fled to the countryside, the death toll this time was less than two hundred.

Contemporary newspaper reports carried stories highlighting the defiance and courage of ordinary Belfast citizens, retelling episodes of the 'business as usual' attitude that has come to define the wider Blitz spirit. On 7 May, for example, the *Northern Whig* featured Wesley Montgomery, 'one of the heroic fire-fighters' who extinguished two incendiary bombs at a first aid post by climbing onto the roof 'with indefatigable zeal'.

Throughout the summer regular press reports made much of the efforts to restore Belfast to its normal appearance as rescue and demolition squads pulled down ruins of commercial premises and private homes. But in truth the May raid had taken a heavy toll on the city centre, with Donegall Place, High Street, Royal Avenue and even the iconic City Hall suffering significant damage. It would take years to repair and rebuild.

Lady Lilian Spender
Stormont, east Belfast

Sunday May 4th was the first day of Double Summer Time and we all had a very late breakfast, and to church. It was a halcyon day, a light frost early and very hot later, with a drenching dew and a lovely tang in the air. The *Magnolia Stellata* bushes have been a sight this year, one mass of shining white, till the night frosts shrivelled them.

We were in the garden all day, and that night we had our second blitz, much worse than the one before, and a lot of damage done in our neighbourhood. We were very lucky to have nothing worse than three broken windows. We also had no gas or electricity, and for the next few days all our cooking had to be done on the tiny open grate in the maid's sitting-room.

Luckily our water was unaffected so, as we have a coke-burning circulator in the kitchen, we have plenty of hot water. There was a terrible lot of damage done to shops and houses in the city, and standing in the garden the morning after, between 4 and 5 a.m., when a despatch rider came to see Wolf, one saw the sky all lit up with a red and angry glare.

William McCready
Librarian
Keadyville Avenue, Whiteabbey

It began about 11.15 p.m. or perhaps 11.30 p.m. The sirens began their weird howling, and I went upstairs to the attic, and opened the skylight right over against the roof. There, looking out, I saw something like the powerful headlights of a car shining straight down from the sky. I couldn't understand it, and inside I had a sinking feeling. I realised that on this occasion the Germans meant business. More and more flares, intensely white, appeared in the sky and soon the whole city was as bright as day. During this time one could hear the steady drone of planes high overhead.

In the streets cars were being driven at great speed, ARP [Air Raid Precautions] and fire-fighting men dashing to their posts whilst others were getting to hell out of the city and into the country. The steady, almost monotonous drone of the planes went on and on; more and more brilliantly white flares came gliding down. Some of them looked like huge lights suspended from overhead wires. It was now after midnight and so bright that I could quite easily read the very small print on a Woodbine packet.

Moya Woodside
Elmwood Avenue, south Belfast

Sirens went at midnight and at 12.30 it started. I stayed in bed till the noise became too shattering, and then put on slacks and dressing gown and came down to join the maid in the kitchen. We got under the table with pillows, rugs and eiderdowns and stayed there, uncomfortable, cold and scared, till about 4.30 a.m. How boring it is – unutterably boring – thus to spend one's nights. Bombs and barrage both were louder and nearer than on the 15th but perhaps sounded worse in the imagination, as windows and roof remained intact.

Patrick Shea
Elmwood Avenue, south Belfast

The bombardment was under way for some time when the sound of a descending footstep on the stairs brought us all to silence. We had forgotten about our air raid warden who I shall call Mr Smith. He had come to us when his firm had transferred him from Dublin to Belfast and his family had, wisely, decided not to move under the conditions then prevailing. Their loss was certainly not our gain. To call Smith a bore would be an understatement. Even the most tolerant, forgiving and patient amongst us (and in every large household there are such people) found him unendurable. But, to his credit, he had volunteered for service as a part-time air raid warden and now he was going out to do his duty. As we heard the front door close behind him there was a general murmur of sympathy not, I regret to say, untinged with relief.

Doreen Bates
Tax Inspector
Sydenham, east Belfast

I caught the 6.00 p.m train from Dublin and came from Belfast by tram reaching the house at 11.55. Three quarters of an hour later the siren went and I felt the contrast between peace and war in all its force.

It was the worst Blitz I have experienced. Our side of the river got it this time (while the other side got it on Easter Tuesday). The half hour from 1.00 a.m. was the worst. We were in the dining room and the windows were blown out; I saw a piece of wood fly across the room and huge clouds of soot and smoke from the fire, before the gas went out. We migrated to my sitting room (which has three inside walls – I had selected it as the safest room in the house before and it was the only room with unbroken windows next day). We had an oil lamp as the fire has not been lighted. The ceiling of the larder and some moulding from my bedroom ceiling came down. The noise was terrific. It went on without a lull at all til 2.30 and gradually abated til 4.00. We went to bed at ten to five with the sky light with fires.

Emma Duffin
Voluntary Aid Detachment Commandant
Stranmillis Military Hospital, soouth Belfast

On Sunday May 4th we had our second 'Blitz'. I do not know how the others re-acted but having seen those pathetic streets, smashed to dust, those distorted bodies, the horror was brought home to me more, but I'm glad to say, though I felt horrified, I did not feel fear. None of the VADs [Voluntary Aid Detachment] nor maids showed signs of panic, though I sensed a slight shudder as bomb after bomb dropped. The barrage this time was terrific. We soon realised it was an even worse 'Blitz' than the last ...

Occasionally I went up the stairs into the hall, to see the VAD patients on stretchers there. The great hall door shuddered and shook in the 'blast' but stood fast. One of the orderlies asked me would I like to look out of the windows where the fire watchers were. He led me along a dark passage. I looked with something like despair at the town. The sky was red above it, great clouds of smoke rose eddying and billowing from the direction of the Lough. I thought of the people who had already endured the last 'Blitz', cowering in terror in the shelters in the already shattered areas.

William McCready
Librarian
Keadyville Avenue, Whiteabbey

About 01.15 it really started. A roar followed by a heavy dull thud and then the sounds of vibrating windows and doors. Then the anti-aircraft guns opened up, and intermittently the sound of heavy guns, stationed all over the city, could be heard.

I came down from the attic to the kitchen and dressed in my overcoat and with my hat on my head, sat down on the settee. The girls were on the floor underneath the heavy oak table. A large piece of plaster fell from the ceiling on top of me. Isobel told me to get into the coal hole under the stairs and there I sat for a long while, bombs falling every few minutes.

Suddenly one, much nearer than the other, blew the kitchen window in with such terrific force. Soon after this we heard whistling bombs: the sound of these missiles was terrifying. Each one seemed to be directed straight to the roof of the house, and all this time, between the nearby sounds of bombs falling, the drone of the German planes, high in the sky, went on and on.

Clonard Community Chronicle
Clonard Monastery, west Belfast
5 May 1941

Another very heavy air raid last night. The Crypt under the sanctuary, also the cellar under the working sacristy, has been fitted out and is opened to the people (women and children only) as an air raid shelter. This act of ours has been very much appreciated by all, Protestants included. Prayers are said and hymns sung by the occupants during the bombing. The fathers and brothers go to the kitchen cellar.

Very heavy bombs destroyed much of the commercial business of the city in this raid. In no raid so far has any Catholic Church been touched. *Deo gratias et Mariae.*

Unnamed German radio reporter
News Bulletin
Deutschlander (German Radio Station)
5 May 1941, 7 p.m.

When I saw Belfast I revised all my ideas about the effects of German bombing. I can really say that I could not believe my eyes. When we approached the target at half-past two we stared silently into a sea of flames such as none of us had seen before. Then after some time our squadron leader, who had already made more than one hundred flights, said 'one would not believe it'. A short time ago we saw Plymouth and Liverpool; the night before was still fresh in our memory.

But in Belfast there was not a large number of conflagrations, but just one enormous conflagration which spread out over the entire harbour and industrial area. Visibility was wonderful, and in the clear moonlight the hundreds of machines which had been there before us could make out their target perfectly. I could not see one fire of any importance in the outer districts of the town, but within the target area there was not one black spot. In the district of the docks, wharves, factories and stockhouses, an area of about one and a half sq kilometres, was on fire.

Here were the large shipbuilding yards, an English shipbuilding centre. Here was the last hideout place for unloading war material from the USA. Here the English had concentrated an important part of their war industries because they thought themselves safe far up in the north, safe from the blows of the German Air Force. This has come to an end. Against the sea of flames one can see the black skeletons of burnt out factories; one can see the burning silos and tall buildings. An enormous black pall of smoke hangs over Belfast.

We calculated that the height of this pall of smoke, which we had already observed from the West coast of England, at over 4,000 metres. AA [anti-aircraft] defence were almost completely silenced, surprised by the power of our attack. Not more than two or three batteries were in action. Their erratic and nervous firing completed the picture of destruction, which nobody will forget.

PC Herbie Ross
Glenravel Street RUC Station

After dark, German aircraft arrived from the Bangor direction. These planes did not drop bombs but released thousands of light balloons which hung in the sky lighting up the city as clear as daylight. These planes were known as Pathfinders. Gunfire on the ground was active but was unable to put out the lights. In a short time the noise of heavy aircraft could be heard approaching the city from the same direction as the Pathfinders.

Soon the heavy bombers were all over the city dropping bombs. The dining area of Glenravel Street RUC station had been reinforced so as it could be used as an air raid shelter. Nine of us sat down on the floor side by side under trestle tables in a single row. After a time the Station was hit by a bomb and the building collapsed over the tables. Pete Lemon spoke and said to me 'we are badly trapped, we will hardly get out alive'. Shortly after that another bomb landed close by and we were covered with more rubble and I remember getting a mouthful of dirty, limey water apparently coming from a huge water tank at the rear of the Station. I was able to speak to Pete but he never replied. I could hear some of my comrades' voices shouting, but that only lasted for a minute or so, and that is when I thought we all might die.

I must have panicked at that stage as I thought I was in a deep valley and that a river on top had burst its banks and was filling the valley with water and that I was going to drown.

We were all dug out some time later – I don't know how long it took … [and] I was treated in the Mater Hospital and at a nursing home near North Queen Street.

Norman Kennedy
Holywood Arches, east Belfast

We were back at school about ten days, that was the big fire storm and my father brought me out from under the stairs to see the school burning down. Horrendous, and the noise of the bombs and sparks of the flames. As soon as sirens would have gone, I got up, put on the good blue suit and was put in charge of the tin box which had the insurance papers, house papers. My mother said she smelt gas and said she'd rather be blown up than gassed so we went into the air raid shelter just round in Crystal St.

Two bombs landed virtually in the same crater and our house disappeared. Easter Tuesday had frightened a lot of people so those remaining were in the air raid shelter and the scene of those bombs I live with yet. 'Abide with Me' got a good rattle and hymns were given out as a belt and braces kind of thing.

Emma Duffin
Voluntary Aid Detachment Commandant
Stranmillis Military Hospital, south Belfast

About 4 o'clock it ended and we came back to the quarters. The smell of burning was in the air, the grass was strewn with … papers. There was a sheet from some child's essay book. On the top page I read 'The End of the World'.

A view of the devastation caused at Bridge Street in Belfast city centre, 4/5 May 1941.

It seemed appropriate. This was the end of the world as we knew it ...

Hospital work had to go on in spite of blitzes and some casualties had been brought in. The maids were wonderful. Somehow breakfast was got on the table at 7 a.m. as usual. I arranged for the maids to go off in relays, and rest as much as possible. I went to Donegall Rd Hospital, calling at Summer Hill and Riddell Hall, to find all well, except both the maids had fled. ...

This time tremendous damage had been done, but more in the shopping centres and though it looked much worse, there were not so many lives lost.

Patrick Shea
Elmwood Avenue, south Belfast

Because I had been assigned to special duties connected with emergency situations, I had been prohibited from joining any of the Civil Defence services. When the All Clear sounded I made my way to the city centre, past burning buildings, through streets criss-crossed with fire hoses, around areas in which unexploded bombs had been found, to the Law Courts which had been designated as the meeting place for the emergency group. From the roof of the building, as the dawn broke, I watched the city centre being consumed in flames and down below, where I stood, open vehicles were bringing dead bodies into St. George's Market.

Major Seán O'Sullivan
Air Raid Precautions observer from Dublin
Monday 5 May 1941

The Officers proceeded by car, leaving Dublin at approx 2.30 a.m and arrived at ARP [Air Raid Precautions] Control Belfast at 5.45 a.m.

Conditions prior to air raid

It was stated that a smoke screen was again in use but owing to weather conditions it was doubtful if it was thoroughly effective as the attack was made during a period of almost dead calm.

Warning

The 'Red' warning was received at 12.15 p.m. and approx half an hour elapsed before the raid commenced. In the interim it was stated that people left their homes and went into the country. The attack lasted for approx two hours.

Number of Attacking Aircraft

There were four distinct waves of attack and estimates of attacking aircraft varying from 60 to 80 bombers.

Type of Attack

In the main the attack was mainly of an incendiary character and although it is stated that quite a large number of HE's [high explosive bombs] were used the evidence of this was not particularly noticeable. The incendiary effect of the attack was, however, all too noticeable and sixty or more major fires resulted. In the central city area many shops were completely burned out and, in the great majority of cases, whole blocks of premises had been reduced to smouldering ruins by 7 a.m. It was apparent that where the fire secured a good initial hold nothing could save the premises involved from complete destruction and all that could be hoped from the fire fighting service was the prevention of spread to neighbouring buildings. The dead calm which prevailed materially helped and it is quite likely that the damage could easily have been doubled had there been a fresh wind blowing.

Damage
In comparison with the previous raid the damage to property was much heavier as most of the premises involved were of the four or five storey type which must have carried large stocks of commodities. Comparatively speaking the dock area appears to have suffered far less damage than the central city area though it must be admitted that four vessels in the harbour were set on fire and that a considerable amount of damage was done by fire to the H[arland] & W[olff] works. The Victoria Barracks again suffered and it was stated that a number of soldiers had been killed and wounded.

The LMS (Northern Counties) Station and Hotel were completely burned out, while in Victoria Street, York Street, High Street, Donegall Place and neighbouring streets hundreds of premises suffered the same fate. During the day a number of unexploded bombs which, by evening, exceeded forty were reported. In general the HEs used were of a light type and served to emphasise the incendiary characer of the attack.

Casualties
By 4.30 p.m. casualties were reported as

Dead	51
Seriously Wounded	75
Slightly Wounded	326
Total	452

These figures do not include military, police or ARP [Air Raid Precautions].

Public Morale

It was noticable that the panic conditions of the previous raid were absent but numbers of people appeared to be moving out of the city during the succeeding day. By comparison, however, the numbers appear to be exceedingly small.

Control and Operation of Service

The telephone system completely broke down early in the raid and this must have had a very serious effect on communications generally. As a result a large number of military depatch riders were allotted for duty at ARP [Air Raid Precautions] headquarters. Control and communications appear to have completely broken down while the control of the fire services was entirely chaotic at 6 a.m. This was apparently due to the fact that the senior officer of the fire service had been injured and neither his second or third officers appeared to be willing to assume control. As a result four of our fire crews and engines were 'standing to' at fire headquarters for more than an hour while Commandant Lawlor and myself endeavoured to secure a detail for them.

It was also evident that the operation of the control centre broke down at many points and the admission of members of ARP services generally in the control room could have had no other result. It was apparent that the fire watching service, if any such exists in Belfast, was an entire failure as there was no evidence of incendiary fires being tackled and subdued in their incipient stages. It is possible that with a well-organised and determined fire watching service a large percentage of the damage by fire would have been avoided.

Holy Family Parish Chronicle
Newington Avenue, north Belfast

We had our second air raid in Belfast and again the parish of Holy Family was almost the centre of the raid. Fortunately no deaths occurred in the parish – although the Church suffered the loss of the middle stained window in the end of the church.

This was caused by high-explosive bombs in Parkend St and in Mountcollyer St. Several houses in Pacific Avenue were burned and incendiary bombs which fell in the Church grounds were extinguished by the priests.

Moya Woodside
Elmwood Avenue, south Belfast

Again this part of town has been lucky, electricity off but gas and water OK. The yard and garden are littered with burnt paper, ashes, bits of shrapnel etc. There is a smell of burning everywhere, everyone looks and feels worn out. This lack of sleep, plus nervous strain, so so exhausting. Went to Welfare office but found nothing to do. Our staff all there, but no applicants.

No trams – crowds walking and many weary faces. Saw several women garbed in slacks and fur coats, looking very strange in the beautiful May sunshine. One can't believe to look at green trees and white blossom and birds singing that these nights of horror are not some evil dream.

Reverend J.B. Woodburn
Moderator of the Presbyterian General Assembly

On Monday morning after the big blitz of Sunday night, I was inexpressibly shocked by the sight of people I saw walking

St Matthew's Church on the Newtownards Road in east Belfast after the May Blitz.

in the streets. I have been working nineteen years in Belfast, and I never saw the like of this before, wretched people, very undersized and underfed, down-and-out looking men and women. They had been bombed out of their homes somewhere, and were wandering the streets.

I ask again, is it creditable to us that there should be such people in a Christian country, and why are they here?

St Matthew's Parish Chronicle
Newtownards Road, east Belfast

Had the heaviest Blitz of all last night. The German planes came over the Dock and City area in continuous waves from midnight till 5 a.m. dropping bombs and incendiaries. The centre of the city was an 'inferno'. A landmine dropped close to St Matthew's Church, at the junction of Newtownards Rd and Bryson St, scattering a large section of the stone plinth and railings. The Church received three incendiary bombs, one behind the Tower, which was extinguished by two soldiers on duty, and others were dealt with by our own Aid Post.

After the All Clear, and after our terrific night's experience, we ventured out to see how our people fared. We found them safe, though shocked by their awful experience. Some streets above St Matthew's were wiped out, and many killed, but not ours. Strange to say, not one of our parishioners was injured, though many about Middlepath and Foundry Sts lost their homes.

Doreen Bates
Tax Inspector
Sydenham, east Belfast

We awoke at 9.00 a.m. though I only had 2½ hours sleep. Owing to the lack of current the All Clear never sounded. People gradually emerged from shelters or were bombed out and there was a lot of noise, so that it was difficult to get any sleep. Before I slept I heard the bird's dawn chorus – a miracle of sanity and sweetness after pandemonium.

For breakfast we had to boil tea on the oil stove, an orange and some cornflakes. I was wise enough to make some sandwiches for lunch, thinking correctly that it would be impossible to get anything in the city. We could get no bread whatever, no milk or tea on the office. The heating and lighting were off by the afternoon, no water.

I was lucky to get a lift in a warden's car to the city, a point normally less than ten mins from the office. I saw appalling destruction of houses and shelters – a church completely demolished but I was told the casualties were less heavy than before as so many people had been in the woods and hills. It took me half an hour to reach the office from the car as I had to get round an area of fires, many still burning and kept getting turned aside.

The opposite side of Donegall Place from the office was hopelessly damaged especially a still burning mackintosh shop and factory which smelt foul. The road was cordoned off and I had several arguments with soldiers and wardens before I was able to reach the office. I found people in the office exchanging stories but no-one seemed to have been hurt though several were bombed out.

I was greeted with some relief as it was known that Sydenham district had had it badly. From 12.30 – 1.30 we had an alert, presumably reconnaissance. I went home by train – four minutes travelling but forty minutes on the station before getting away though so far as I could see the railway was untouched. I saw only one shop open in the city, a little greengrocers where I bought a lettuce.

Moya Woodside
Elmwood Avenue, south Belfast
6 May 1941

What a day yesterday was. I don't think I have ever been so tired in all my life. In the afternoon I had to fetch an elderly bombed-out refugee couple (wife an invalid) from the man's downtown office and bring them here. I couldn't get the car anywhere near the office, as the road was roped off, and all around were still-burning buildings and crashing walls. It is rather terrifying to suddenly find one's own familiar town looking like photographs of Madrid or Barcelona. One has the impression that everything is unreal.

Rescued my refugees who were brave, but in a terrifyingly nervous condition – and then the problem – where to put them at night? They would not stay here (we are not a mile from the centre of the town), knew no-one in the country, and talked hysterically of spending the night in the fields. I rang up everybody I could think of but to no avail. All were away, full up, 'phone out of order, or stalled at the idea of giving shelter to partially helpless woman. A phone call to one of our committee members in the country was not accepted by the Exchange – 'only calls of national importance are being taken' I was told.

By this time it was 6 p.m. and I was beginning to feel quite frantic. What on earth could I do with them? As a last resort, I took the car and went to try another committee member living in another town. She wasn't in, but her husband came to the rescue and offered them temporary shelter in the factory where he works, right in the country. I could have embraced him on the spot! Took them out after supper and fixed them up where there was at least peace if not comfort. Home to bed at 9 p.m. more dead than alive. Sirens went again at 11 p.m. but I didn't get up. Felt so tired I didn't care what happened. There was another raid but shorter and not so fierce. Over about 3.30 a.m.

Went to town on bicycle to do some shopping. Belfast will certainly never look the same again. I should say that one third of the entire centre of town has gone, streets littered with glass, water, and debris. Many roped off and firemen still working on smoking buildings. Crowds standing about, many appearing to be employees or owners of shops and offices which don't exist any more. It is curious how fire damage seems to leave less than bombs. One would expect some floors still to be standing, with mounds of unburnable stuff at the bottom, but of burnt-out buildings nothing remains but twisted girders, and some outside walls.

My fish-shop was some way down the roped-off main street, but the assistants were there, and walked up and down to the barrier talking orders and carrying lots of fish for inspection. This would have been very amusing if the scenes round about weren't so awful. A very young and rustic soldier was guarding the barrier and engaged in constant altercations with people wishing to pass through to their still standing offices. They were irate and desperate, and he was hot and embarrassed and plainly fed-up with repeating his orders and chasing after those who tried to slip past.

The tale of Monday night's havoc is not yet told (probably censorship prevents me from giving even a scant account here.) Less people were killed than in the previous blitz, as this one was mainly directed on the city centre and shipyards, but we now have an unemployment problem of staggering proportions. Thousands and thousands are walking the streets, with only the faintest hope of being employed again till after the war. What is going to become of these people, many of them homeless and bereaved (or they will be) as well as without work?

At present this side of things has scarcely been realised, but material repair or reconstruction is of small importance besides this human problem.

Press reports of the raids are nauseating. Of course they are hampered by not being allowed to mention any street or building by name, but even so it shouldn't be necessary to turn out all the journalistic cliché and claptrap about 'stricken mothers', 'citizens', 'courage and stoicism', 'traders carrying on with a smile' etc etc. Truth is that people are dazed, worn-out, many despairing, nerves and instability everywhere, evacuation and rest centres a mess of conflicting instructions and overwhelmed by sheer numbers; thousands walk out of town every night to sleep in the fields and suburbs, local authorities were almost totally unprepared to cope with such a situation. (As I was one of the ones who wishful-thinkingly held the theory we wouldn't be bombed, I am in no position to criticise. The foregoing is merely a statement of fact.)

At weekly refugee (German and Austrian) case committee, the repercussions were already in evidence. How to evacuate or find billets for bombed-out refugees, some in ill-health, how to find new employment for those whose employers have departed to the country or whose place or work has been destroyed: how to convince the nervous and neurotic ones that if they are not actually homeless they must 'stay put' (and be it remembered that all these people are under a nervous strain already) – such are some of our problems, not made any easier by the knowledge of a dwindling bank balance and no hope of raising fresh funds.

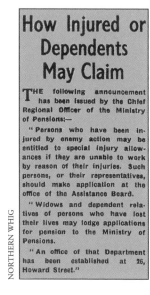

How Injured or Dependents May Claim

THE following announcement has been issued by the Chief Regional Officer of the Ministry of Pensions:—

" Persons who have been injured by enemy action may be entitled to special injury allowances if they are unable to work by reason of their injuries. Such persons, or their representatives, should make application at the office of the Assistance Board.

" Widows and dependent relatives of persons who have lost their lives may lodge applications for pension to the Ministry of Pensions.

" An office of that Department has been established at 26, Howard Street."

NORTHERN WHIG

Sir Wilfrid Spender
Head of the Northern Ireland Civil Service
8 May 1941

Immediately after the last heavy Blitz the Prime Minister called me up urgently on the telephone to speak about the protection of Carson's statue. I feel sure that Carson himself would not have wished this matter to be regarded as one of major importance in existing conditions. I have suggested to the Prime Minister that the large crater caused by the 600lb bomb about one hundred yards from Carson's statue shows that the risk of damage is comparatively small and that I do not think any adequate steps can be taken except to remove the statue from its present site.

Doreen Bates
Tax Inspector
Sydenham, east Belfast
7 May 1941

Belfast has begun to return to normal, more quickly than after Easter Tuesday. Buses, few and sporadic, were running on much diverted routes but I managed to go and come fairly well. The Bennetts called in the evening. They had had to leave their home for twenty-four hours owing to a mystery hole nearby. She had been sick and couldn't eat anything. Mr B told a gloomy tale of the shipyard, the famous ropeworks had a large fire. Apparently the power station was not damaged much as electricity was on last night. The gasworks are intact but the mains are destroyed so we are still without gas.

On the Antrim side of the river, services are normal. The Telegraph office was packed and telegrams were being accepted only at sender's risk. No English papers since Sunday and the shop where I am registered for bacon and cheese and jam has disappeared.

8 May 1941

Today the inconveniences following the air raid were more in evidence than ever. Some of the office building had to be evacuated because adjacent buildings were being dynamited. Our windows at the back were blown out; water was turned off in the city all day as well as still being off in Sydenham … traffic more congested than ever. Spent most of lunchtime going the Food Office to ask where to get rations of cheese, bacon and jam now that my shop is burnt down. I was given four alternative shops and got some bacon after a long wait at Liptons. Also for the first time in NI I got lamb cutlets for my meat ration.

German Radio Report
10 May 1941, 21.30

German reconnaissance planes have flown over Belfast and taken photographs from which it can be seen that during the attack on Belfast on the night of 4th May by the German Air Force, hits were scored on three vessels in Belfast shipyards. The vessels are a tanker of about 10,000 tons and two merchant vessels of about 8,000 tons and 7,000 tons respectively. Three vessels, which were nearly ready, were totally destroyed.

1941 Register of Crimes, County of Belfast
Belfast E District
12 May 1941, between 6 a.m. and 7 p.m.

Abraham I., 34 yrs, soldier, arrested for looting. Accused entered eight houses that had been damaged as a result of enemy action and stole £4-7-0 in coppers from the gas meters.

At City Commission on 28th July 1941 accused pleaded guilty and was sentenced to eighteen months hard labour.

Moya Woodside
Elmwood Avenue, south Belfast
3 June 1941

Only now, three weeks after the Blitz, are steps being taken to distribute the money raised then (some thousands) for a Distress Fund. Potential recipients will be lucky if they receive anything before August, as forms must be filled in, investigations made and a special committee deliberate on each case. I have started interviewing people today at the Welfare Office for this Fund, and think that while undoubtedly there is much genuine need, one of the biggest jobs is going to be eliminating the 'scroungers'. Those who have suffered least are the most talkative and the hardest to deal with.

4 June 1941

Visited a woman in the Poor Law Infirmary who has been there since April 15th Blitz, suffering from burns and a broken leg. All of her four children had been killed, but she was still in ignorance of this and believed them to have been evacuated. The Sister told me that the woman's husband has not plucked up courage to tell her yet; and that he was supposed to have returned to work in England last Saturday.

[She] described her experiences to me, saying how the last thing she remembered was being pinned under a mass of bricks and hearing the children screaming that they were being burnt. Curiously enough, she scarcely made any enquiries about them, which made the interview much easier than I had anticipated.

I then visited another woman who was temporarily living in a good working-class district, having been bombed out of her own home. She told me that the day following the first raid, she gave birth to a five month's old child (which of course died) and the same night got up and trailed to the field with her other three children; and continued doing this for nearly a week till she was taken in at a Rest Centre. Result: she is going into hospital for a repair operation, and has been told her health will never be the same again.

And then I think of people I know with cars and friends and house in the country, who have comfortably evacuated themselves and now complain loudly of inconvenience or slow trains or a few broken windows.

5 June 1941

Coming home last night about 11.30 p.m. from visiting a friend in the suburbs, I saw several parties of people walking out towards the end of the tram lines, carrying rugs and blankets. This, a month after our last raid.

9 June 1941

Felt that I am being some use at last. Spent from 10.00 a.m. to 1.00 p.m. interviewing as fast as I could go for the city Distress Fund. People kept popping into the chair in front of me the minute it was vacated, while rows and rows waited patiently (or impatiently) behind them. I kept thinking 'so this is what it feels like to be a civil servant' but actually I quite enjoy being busy, even in this sort of rush. Most frequent was 'we couldn't stick it' (i.e. life in the country) or 'we couldn't afford the fares'. People generally seem keen to return to their houses, even in vulnerable areas. One man told me that for the last few months he had been earning an average of £8 weekly as a bricklayer, (wages normally £4 plus overtime) but since being injured in the raid his income had dropped to 38/- compensation. I had a number of cases of this sort of thing, where perhaps four or five in the house had been earning good money and living in accordance; and are now all out of work, some with no prospect of re-employment till the war is over.

11 June 1941

Interviewing again for the Distress Fund. One woman opened her shawl and showed us a horrible sight – a premature baby, looking like something out of an anatomical museum, with yellow face and dying of jaundice. She was quite matter-of-fact about it, and said her last baby had been the same and had died in three weeks. She didn't think it was 'worthwhile bothering' to take it to hospital.

Northern Whig
13 June 1941

Evidence of how whole families were wiped out in the air raids of April 15th to 16th were given yesterday at an inquiry by the City Coroner (Dr H.P. Lowe) into the presumed deaths of fifty-four people missing since the raid. The inquiry was held in the City Hall, and in each case a verdict of 'presumed dead' was returned.

Sympathy with the bereaved and homeless was expressed by the Coroner, who testified to the bravery and efficiency of the ARP [Air Raid Precautions] and AFS [Auxiliary Fire Service]. How a family of seven were wiped out at 142 Duncairn Gardens, was told by James Warwick, a brother of Nathaniel B. Warwick, who was killed with his wife, four daughters and one son.

Mrs H. Dornan, of Vicarfield St in Glasgow, another victim, was on a visit to her daughter and grand-daughter Mrs Lorna McNeill and Miss H. McNeill, 65 Hogarth St, who were also killed. It was stated that their own home was almost intact but that they had gone to a house opposite for company.

Eight members of a family named Wilson were killed when a bomb wrecked their house in Edlingham Street, while in Hogarth St ten members of the Gordon family were wiped out.

Irish News
14 June 1941

The first mass inquest on air raid victims in NI was held in the City Hall yesterday, by H.P. Lowe, City coroner. The inquiry concerned the fate of fifty-four persons reported missing after a six-hour raid on April 15/16 1941. In each case death was presumed. Among the victims were two families of eight, and one of seven.

Many tragic stories were told by relatives in their evidence and in some cases a scrap of paper or an insurance book were the only evidence of identity. In several cases the victims had left their homes to seek refuge with neighbours and had been killed while their own homes had remained intact.

Sarah and Mary Addis, 23 Sheridan St, had been asked by a neighbour if they were all right. They said there were but that they were very nervous. The neighbour brought the two women into her home and shortly afterwards both families perished while the house collapsed.

It was stated by a relative that Stephen Brown and his wife Sarah, whose home at 267 York St received a direct hit, had just returned home after visiting their four children whom they had evacuated to Aughnacloy.

Mrs Margaret Sweeney said she was the daughter of Thomas Gordon and Elizabeth Gordon, 29 Hogarth St. They lived with their sons, William and Hugh Gordon and their daughters Georgina and Kathleen. On the morning after the raid, the witness went to her parents home but could find no trace of her father, mother, brothers and sisters. Another brother and his wife, Samuel and Susan Gordon, who lived at Greenmount St, were also unable to be traced. Witness went to the street every day for news of her people but the chief warden assured her the search was hopeless.

A tragic story was told of Mary Henry and her aunt, Susan Henry of 24 Dawson St, who were coming from the GNR [railway] when the raid started. They were invited to take shelter in a house, 26 Unity Street, occupied by a family called Donnelly. The house received a direct hit and the entire family of five Donnellys were wiped out, Mary and Susan Henry perishing with them.

One of the saddest stories of the inquest related to the Warwick family whose house at 142 Duncairn Gardens received a direct hit. This killed the father, Nathaniel Warwick, the mother Alicia and daughters Joanne, Mildred, Nan and Winifred and a son Nathaniel who was fifteen years of age. One family crossed the road to safety where they were killed, their own house being preserved. They were Mrs Lorna McNeill and Miss H. McNeill of 65 Hogarth Street.

Moya Woodside
Elmwood Avenue, south Belfast
20 June 1941

Out in Blitz slum district this morning, viewing houses where people are billeted (for Government Welfare Authority). The place is still in a terrible mess, with whole slabs of street lying in disorderly ruins. Not much chance of forgetting things if you lived there, I thought. Surprising how many children and young babies were still about.

This sort of billeting, where inhabitants of one street have been billeted with the next or nearby, and where habits and standards of living are similar, is obviously much more successful than the transfer to the suburbs. The women I interviewed (both hostess and visitor) all expressed themselves as 'getting on alright' and in many cases had been friends or known to each other since before the raid.

In one house, two boys of school age were sitting about looking half-dead. On asking why they weren't at school I was told 'Oh, they often sleep in now. We always sit up til about 2.30 a.m. Everybody round here does the same, so we have plenty of company.'

The word 'billettee' is bad enough, but one of the clerks at the Welfare Office started talking about 'billitor'. I positively squirmed!

Irish News
22 June 1941

The harrowing story of how sixteen people, a family of ten and another of six, were killed in a house in Ballynure Street, Belfast, when the house was bombed during the Easter Tuesday air raid, was told at the inquest yesterday into the deaths of fifty-two missing people whom the Coroner certified as 'presumed dead'. At a similar inquest last week fifty-four people were presumed dead.

An atmosphere of tragedy surrounded the proceedings as the surviving relatives and friends told of whole families being wiped out by high explosive bombs.

The tragic story concerning the deaths of the occupants of No. 4 Ballynure Street, which received a direct hit, was told by James Clarke of Henderson Avenue who lost his father, a Post Office official, his mother, six brothers, a sister and a niece. He said he had identified the body of his mother but although he had searched for the others, he could not find any trace of them.

In the same house were the wife and five children of William Douglas, a solider. All were killed. Mr Douglas told the Coroner that his family lived at 8 Ballynure Street and had taken refuge in No. 4. Only one child, who was in Groomsport at the time, was left. He had identified the bodies of his wife and three children but could find no trace of his sons, James and Samuel.

Eleven people were killed at No. 3 Torrens Road. Eight of them had left their own homes to shelter in the house which was later demolished by a direct hit. The dead were Mrs

A.K. Kelly, her son and daughter; Mrs Annie Mallon and her three children and Mrs Grace Knight, her sons, Arthur and James and her daughter Mildred.

Mr Arthur Knight said he was away at work on the night of the raid and he had not seen any of his family since. All of them are gone, he said. The Coroner – If you had not gone to work you would probably be gone too. Mr Knight – I wish I had been with them.

Eight people perished at 95 Blythe Street. Mr Cooke said he and his wife and children left their home, 184 Blythe Street, to go to No. 98. His wife suggested that he should light the fire in their own house and he went out to do so. As he was returning to number 95 the bomb fell. All were wiped out in the house but, ironically, No. 184 was undamaged.

A bus driver, John Burns, who lodged at 10 Percy Street, told the Coroner how three widows at this address met their deaths in the house. Mr Burns said the three women were sheltering in the coal-hole when a bomb exploded. Three were killed at 49 Veryan Gardens, Whitewell. They were Mrs McKay and her baby and Miss Susan Doherty, a grandchild.

At the state of the inquiry, all present, at the request of the Coroner, stood as a mark of respect to the victims

London Gazette
16 September 1941

Awarded the George Medal
William Brett, Constable, Royal Ulster Constabulary.
Alexander McCusker, Constable, Royal Ulster Constabulary.

Constables McCusker and Brett were engaged in extinguishing incendiary bombs when a high explosive bomb fell nearby and they were buried by debris from falling buildings. Constable McCusker was blown through a door into a house. He managed to extricate himself and rescued a boy. Constable Brett joined McCusker and both men, though injured and suffering from shock, began rescue work and continued until help arrived. The two Constables displayed bravery and devotion to duty in face of great danger.

19 September 1941

Awarded the George Medal
Robert Moore, Constable, Royal Ulster Constabulary.

Awarded the British Empire Medal (Civil Division)
Alfred King, Constable, Royal Ulster Constabulary.

A six-storey building was hit by bombs and collapsed onto some small houses. Many people were injured and trapped and a Police squad was sent to help with rescue operations. Constable Moore dug away debris and sawed through planks and rescued a man and his wife and child. Later, with Constable King, he went to a house where people were trapped. They saw a hole in the debris which had apparently been the stairway to the top of the house, but the stairway had collapsed and the walls on both sides, which were about three feet apart, were cracked and likely to cave in at any moment. Although warned of the danger, Constable King volunteered to descend and by his efforts succeeded in bringing the casualties to safety. Constable Moore then went to another house which had been wrecked and helped to release a woman from under a beam. He dug down about six feet and found a little girl, aged about eleven years. Her clothes were on fire. The Constable got her out of the flames and extinguished the burning clothing with his hands, sustaining severe burns whilst so doing. Constable Moore showed outstanding gallantry and total disregard of personal safety and with Constable King was responsible for saving many lives.

28 October 1941

Awarded the British Empire Medal (Civil Division)

William John Ford, Bomb Identification Officer, Civil Defence Service, Belfast.

William Ernest Bennett, Messenger, Civil Defence Wardens Service.

Bombs destroyed a number of houses and fractured a gas main. Ford and Bennett burrowed a way under the debris and, working in a prone position, made a tunnel six yards long. They reached an elderly man who was trapped and, by taking the weight of the debris on their backs, they managed to extricate him.

They then climbed through a hole in a partially destroyed staircase and after clearing away debris, succeeded in bringing two women to safety. During this time, bombs were continually falling and there was also danger from collapsing wreckage. Ford and Bennett showed courage and devotion to duty and both suffered from the effects of inhaling coal gas.

Denise Forster, Auxiliary Nurse, Civil Defence Ambulance Service, Belfast.

When an Ambulance Depot was demolished by a high explosive bomb, Nurse Forster and many of the personnel were buried in the wreckage. Extricating herself with difficulty, she immediately began to release the others. Later she volunteered to go with an ambulance on a particularly dangerous journey through a district which was being heavily attacked with HE [high explosive] and incendiary bombs. Nurse Forster continued to work in the greatest danger throughout the night, refusing to be relieved and only ceased her activities when ordered to do so some hours after the raid was over.

Soldiers enjoy an impromptu organ recital in York Street, Belfast city centre,
15/16 April 1941.

ACKNOWLEDGEMENTS

I am deeply grateful to many people who have helped me during the research for this book; they were all generous with time, advice and practical help. This book is the result of their collective effort. Many individual archive holders and institutions responded to my request for any reference they held to the Belfast Blitz, and they all deserve a special word of thanks.

Aileen McClintock and Anne McVeigh at the Public Record Office of Northern Ireland whose relocation to new premises at Titanic Quarter is testament to Belfast's unique archival heritage and community memory; Diarmuid Kennedy and staff at Special Collections, Queen's University Belfast Library; Fr Gerry McCloskey, Holy Family Parish, Belfast; Rector and Community of Clonard Monastery; the family of the late Nellie Bell; Jonathan Bardon; Gerard McNamee of Saint Malachy's College; Norah Coyle and family; John Killen and Monica McErlane at the Linen Hall Library; the indefatigable John Gray; Valerie Adams from the Presbyterian Historical Society; Sr Lucina Montague; Jimmy Kelly who saw, and reported on, the bonfires on the hillside in April and May 1941; J.M.G. Dickson and Edward McCamley for facilitating a serach in the archive of Belfast Royal Academy; BBC Northern Ireland archive; Margot Neill and the family of the late Moya Woodside, for providing photographs of perhaps the greatest chronicler of the Belfast Blitz; the Estate of Doreen Bates for permission to use her extracts; the Police Service of Northern Ireland Museum, Belfast; the staff at the Somme Heritage Centre Oral History Archive, a resource of international significance, though not yet, alas, of international renown; the executors of the Robert Greacen estate;

Dr Sarah Ferris, for her unrivalled knowledge of all things *McFaddenia*; the University of Sussex and Adam Matthew Digital for permission to access and use extracts from the Mass Observation Survey; Lisa Dolan and her staff at the Irish Military Archives in Cathal Brugha Barracks, Dublin, a treasure trove for understanding twentieth-century Irish history; Fr Robert McCabe CF for his detective work in sourcing more information on Major Seán O'Sullivan; the Imperial War Museum who do so much unacknowledged work to preserve the human memory of conflict.

Appreciation is also expressed to Patsy Horton and staff at Blackstaff Press, still flying the flag for local publishing 'forty years on'.

It hardly needs to be said that any errors are entirely my responsibility.

The editor and publisher gratefully acknowledge permission to include the following copyright material:

Text acknowledgements

1941 REGISTER OF CRIMES, extracts reproduced by kind permission of the Police Museum, Police Service of Northern Ireland.

AIR RAID PRECAUTIONS REPORT, extract reproduced by kind permission of the Public Records Office of Northern Ireland.

AMBROSE, ALFRED, extracts reproduced by kind permission of the Public Records Office of Northern Ireland.

AUSTIN, BILL, extract taken from the Somme Heritage Oral History Archive, and reproduced by kind permission of the Somme Heritage Centre.

by kind permission of the Public Records Office of Northern Ireland.

CLONARD COMMUNITY CHRONICLE, extract reproduced by kind permission of the Redemptorist Community Archives of Clonard Monastery.

DIXON, HUGH, extracts reproduced by kind permission of the Hugh Dixon Estate.

DUFFIN, EMMA, extracts reproduced by kind permission of the Public Records Office of Northern Ireland.

GALLAGHER, REVD ERIC, extract taken from an article which appeared in the *Belfast Telegraph*, April 1971, and reproduced by kind permission of the *Belfast Telegraph*.

GERMAN RADIO REPORT, copyright holder not traced.

GERMAN REPORTER, UNNAMED, copyright holder not traced.

GREACEN, ROBERT, extracts taken from private correspondence to Roy McFadden. Permission granted by the Estate of the late Robert Greacen through the Jonathan Williams Literary Agency.

HARRIS, G.T., extracts taken from the collection of G.T. Harris at the Imperial War Museum, London, copyright holder not traced. The Imperial War Museum would be grateful for any information which might help to trace those whose identities or addresses that are not currently known.

HOLY FAMILY PARISH CHRONICLE, extracts reproduced by kind permission of Father Gerard McCloskey, Administrator, Holy Family.

IRISH NEWS, extracts reproduced with thanks to the *Irish News*.

KELLY, JAMES, extracts taken from *Bonfires on the Hillside: Eyewitness Account of Political Upheaval in Northern Ireland* (1995) and reproduced by kind permission of the author.

KELLY, JOHN, extract taken from an article which appeared in the *Belfast Telegraph*, April 1971, and reproduced by kind permission of the *Belfast Telegraph*.

KENNEDY, NORMAN, extracts taken from the Somme Heritage Oral History Archive, and reproduced by kind permission of the Somme Heritage Centre.

LITTLE, REVD DR JAMES, extract taken from a parliamentary speech given in the House of Commons, 1 April 1941. Parliamentary material is reproduced with the permission of the Controller of HMSO on behalf of Parliament and under the terms of the Open Government Licence for Public Sector Information, http://www.nationalarchives.gov.uk/doc/open-government-licence/open-government-licence.htm.

LONDON GAZETTE, extracts reproduced under the terms of the Open Government Licence for Public Sector Information, http://www.nationalarchives.gov.uk/doc/open-government-licence/open-government-licence.htm

McCREADY, WILLIAM, copyright holder not traced.

McGARVEY, SGT G.A. (Bertie), extract taken from the papers of Miss V.E.E. Cossar at the Imperial War Museum, London, copyright holder not traced. The Imperial War Museum would be grateful for any information which might help to trace those whose identities or addresses that are not currently known.

MacDERMOTT, MAJOR JOHN C., extract taken from Volume 24 (1941, 42) of the Stormont papers (22 April 1941), http://stormontpapers.ahds.ac.uk, and reproduced under the terms of the Open Government Licence for Public Sector Information, http://www.nationalarchives.gov.uk/doc/open-government-licence/open-government-licence.htm

MORROW, JOHN, extract taken from the *Honest Ulsterman* (1989) and reproduced by kind permission of John Morrow, novelist and short story writer.

NORTHERN WHIG AND BELFAST POST, copyright holder not traced.

O'SULLIVAN, MAJOR SEÁN, extracts taken from MA/EDP/40/8 at the Irish Military Archives, Cathal Brugha Barracks, Dublin, and reproduced by kind permission of the Irish Military Archives.

THE OWL, extract taken from the Belfast Royal Academy School Magazine and reproduced by kind permission of Belfast Royal Academy.

PLEYDELL, CAPTAIN M.J., extracts taken from the collection of Captain M.J. Pleydell at the Imperial War Museum, London, copyright holder not traced. The Imperial War Museum would be grateful for any information which might help to trace those whose identities or addresses that are not currently known.

PRINCIPAL TEACHERS' UNION (Minute Book), copyright holder not traced.

ROCKS, IRIS, extract taken from the Somme Heritage Oral History Archive, and reproduced by kind permission of the Somme Heritage Centre.

ROSS, HERBIE, copyright holder not traced.

RYAN, LT G.G., extracts taken from MA/EDP/40/6 at the Irish Military Archives, Cathal Brugha Barracks, Dublin, and reproduced by kind permission of the Irish Military Archives.

ST MATTHEW'S PARISH CHRONICLE, extract reproduced by kind permission of St Matthew's Church.

SHEA, PATRICK, copyright holder not traced.

SPENDER, LADY LILIAN, extracts reproduced by kind permission of the Public Records Office of Northern Ireland.

SPENDER, SIR WILFRID, extracts reproduced by kind permission of the Public Records Office of Northern Ireland.

STANLEY, KEN, extracts taken from the Somme Heritage Oral History Archive, and reproduced by kind permission of the Somme Heritage Centre.

WALSH, JULIA, extract reproduced by kind permission of the Dominican Community, Falls Road.

WOODBURN, REVD J.B., extract taken from a speech given in June 1941 to the Presbyterian Historical Society, and reproduced by kind permission of the General Assembly of the Presbyterian Church in Ireland and the Presbyterian Historical Society.

WOODSIDE, MOYA, extracts taken from MO Diary Number 5462 at the Mass Observation Archive, University of Sussex. Reproduced with permission of Curtis Brown Group Ltd, London on behalf of the Trustees of the Mass Observation Archive. Copyright © The Trustees of the Mass Observation Archive.

Picture acknowledgements

Preliminary material

viii 'Evacuation of School Children', taken from *Belfast News Letter*, 4 July 1940

xii *Moya Woodside*, reproduced by kind permission of the Estate of Moya Woodside.

xvi 'If the Invader Comes', taken from *Belfast News Letter*, 27 July 1940

79 'Children being evacuated at the railway station'
[AR 61], April/May 1941, reproduced by kind
permission of the *Belfast Telegraph*.

83 'Residents of Ballyclare Street salvaging household
effects' [AR 26], 15/16 April 1941, reproduced by
kind permission of the *Belfast Telegraph*.

85 'Billeting of Homeless People', taken from *Belfast
News Letter*, 19 April 1941

92 'Queen's University students demolishing buildings on
Eglinton Street' [AR 69], 4/5 May 1941, reproduced
by kind permission of the *Belfast Telegraph*.

94 'Furniture being removed from houses, Sunningdale
Park' [AR 154], 4/5 May 1941, reproduced by kind
permission of the *Belfast Telegraph*.

95 'Business as Usual', taken from *Belfast News Letter*,
19 April 1941

97 'Belfast Civil Defence Authority', taken from *The
Northern Whig and Belfast Post*, 17 April 1941.
Copyright holder not traced.

102 'Official Notices', taken from *The Northern Whig and
Belfast Post*, 17 April 1941. Copyright holder not
traced.

108 (top) 'Owners or tenants of houses damaged ...';
(bottom) 'Urgent Notice', both taken from
The Northern Whig and Belfast Post, 19 April 1941.
Copyright holder not traced.

114 'Despite the Blitz ...', taken from *Belfast News Letter*,
26 April 1941

116 'Belfast Air Raid Emergency', taken from *The
Northern Whig and Belfast Post*, 17 April 1941.
Copyright holder not traced.

The May Raid

132 'Bridge Street, Belfast' [AR 32], 4/5 May 1941,
reproduced by kind permission of the *Belfast
Telegraph.*

138 'Destruction caused by the Blitz to St Matthew's
Church, Newtownards Road' [AR 166], 4/5 May
1941, reproduced by kind permission of the *Belfast
Telegraph.*

144 'How Injured or Dependents May Claim', taken from
The Northern Whig and Belfast Post, 17 April 1941.
Copyright holder not traced.

156 'Impromptu organ recital, York Street' [AR 192],
15/16 April 1941, reproduced by kind permission of
the *Belfast Telegraph.*

INDEX OF AUTHORS

Numbers in italics refer to illustrations.

INDEX

This index covers places and locations in and around Belfast.
Page numbers in italics refer to illustrations.